3,000 Days in Afghanistan

Fighting Instability, Narcotics, and Poverty in a Dangerous Place

Chris Corsten

Copyright © 2020 Chris Corsten

All rights reserved.

ISBN:

DEDICATION

This book is dedicated to all the men and women who sacrificed their time, effort and lives to help bring hope to the people of Afghanistan. It is also dedicated to my late mother, Marsha Corsten, who passed away in 2019 just before completion of the book.

CONTENTS

	Acknowledgments	i
1	Military	2
2	Counternarcotics	46
3	Transition to Aid Work	74
4	Back to Afghanistan One More Time	137

ACKNOWLEDGMENTS

I would like to thank several people who have helped me with the production of this book. I would like to thank my friends Steve Kling and Bob Huggett for providing pictures and helping to refresh my memory of events. I would like to thank my editor Amy Reid for her time polishing my words. Mostly, I would like to thank my wife, Laura and son, Ryan for allowing me the time to write and putting up with me through the months of effort to get the book completed

BACKGROUND

For nearly two decades, the U.S. and its allies have been engaged in Afghanistan. So many people wonder why we are still there and what exactly we are doing there. I wrote this book to help detail my nearly decade of experience in Afghanistan where I served as a military officer and a civilian working on several U.S. government programs. I wanted to give a sense of some of the successes we had and many of the failures we endured. I hope some of the lessons learned from my experience can help others understand the complexities of living and working in a war zone, and maybe how the U.S. can do a better job the next time our country embarks on a similar adventure.

I was born in 1974 and grew up in the small town of Marinette, Wisconsin. I was raised as a Catholic in small Catholic schools all the way through high school. I was a three-sport athlete and dreamed one day of becoming an Army officer. I had at one time planned to apply to West Point, and had the credentials and ability to do it, but I changed my mind during my senior year and decided to become a chiropractor. I was extremely excited about that as a career and attended Ripon College majoring in biology.

Midway through my sophomore year of college I felt like something was missing, and I wanted to look at the Army officer program again. After some soul searching, I joined the Army ROTC program and became a second lieutenant in the Army at graduation. My plan was to be a reservist and go to chiropractic school right away that fall of 1997. Just before graduation my colonel called me and said he would not sign off on my reserve status since he thought I would be a great active duty officer. We talked for a while, and he said that he would sign off on my reserve status only if I thought about it for a couple of days and let him know if I changed my mind. After doing some thinking, I decided what the hell; I could use some adventure for a couple of years and maybe even save up some money for chiropractic school, which was about $100,000. I called him back the next day and said I would go full-time active duty. At graduation, I became a medical service officer, which dovetailed with my future aspirations to work in the medical field as a chiropractor.

CHAPTER 1. MILITARY

I had a great career as an active-duty officer. I spent my first year in Korea as a staff officer in Seoul. I made some terrific friends and learned to love living overseas. My next assignment was as a platoon leader in the 82nd Airborne Division at Fort Bragg, North Carolina. That was my dream job, and I loved being part of such an elite unit. What young man would not want to jump out of planes and shoot stuff up? As a young officer I definitely had my share of growing pains but learned so much from both the great officers I wanted to emulate and the poor officers that showed me what not to do. Toward the end of my time at Fort Bragg, my battalion was deployed to Kosovo for six months. That experience was an eye-opener, as it was my first time working with civilians in a conflict zone. I saw firsthand ethnic conflict in the villages between ethnic Serbs and ethnic Albanians. I started attending some meetings with local government officials and aid groups, and met some Army guys who worked specifically with the civilian population. They often wore civilian clothes and blended in with the locals. That was a semi-special ops unit called Civil Affairs that intrigued me. It would come back to change my life path later.

After Kosovo, I was promoted to captain, and assigned as a joint staff officer in a unit that oversaw the movement of patients and plans at the highest levels of the military. It was a very boring job but did allow me to constantly travel to Washington, D.C., to the Pentagon; Hawaii; Korea; Japan; and several states. I was rarely home, but when I was I was mostly reviewing doctrine and trying to stay awake at my desk. I started looking for another job in my spare time and found a company command open in Egypt. I called up my branch manager and got accepted for the job.

A month later I was leaving St. Louis for Egypt and was back in command of over 100 troops in the middle of the Sinai Peninsula. It was my first experience with Arab culture, and I enjoyed the heck out of it. My job was command of all troops in charge of medical support to the Multinational Force and Observers, which monitored the peace treaty between Egypt and Israel. At the time, it was the strangest place to be assigned. The Sinai Peninsula was a dry piece of desert separating Egypt from Israel containing only a few small villages, aside from Sharm el Sheik, which was a major party and scuba diving resort town at the bottom of the peninsula. I learned to scuba dive there in the pristine waters of the Red Sea. I also went to Israel several times to visit the Holy Land and party in the beach town of Eilat. I loved that assignment, and it was a fitting end to my active-duty career. I did all that I really wanted to do on the active-duty side and was ready to get on with my goal of becoming a chiropractor.

I started chiropractic college in Daytona Beach, Florida, in the fall of 2004 and continued my Army service by becoming a reserve duty Civil Affairs officer. I knew full on that I would be assigned to either Afghanistan or Iraq at some point in the near future, and figured there would be a year of deployment that would interrupt my studies, but that was no big deal to me. I started school in October, and in January of 2005 I was offered a Civil Affairs team command in Afghanistan, and I took it in a second. I had only finished my first quarter of school and was doing well. I did not know that I would be pulled back to active duty to go to Afghanistan so soon. I also did not know that it would be the start of my near decade of dedication to the Afghanistan cause.

Afghanistan

When I first got the assignment, I did not know anything more about Afghanistan than anyone else. Of course, I knew that Al Qaeda had struck New York City and the Pentagon on 9/11, using Afghanistan as their base. I was also aware that the Taliban, who had been in charge of nearly all of Afghanistan in 2001, had sheltered Al Qaeda. However, I did not know much about the history of Afghanistan prior to 9/11. From the time that the Soviet Union had invaded Afghanistan in 1979 until the present time, Afghanistan has been in a state of conflict. The Mujahedeen fighters pushed the Soviets out in 1989, only to begin a civil war that ended with the Taliban gaining power in 1996. From then until we toppled the Taliban, Afghanistan was ruled under a strict Islamic fundamentalist system. There was little peace or stability in that country for decades.

The new Afghan government, propped up by the U.S. after our invasion in 2001, inherited a country that was completely destroyed in every way. Government and civil society were non-existent, infrastructure was crumbled, and the people were fragmented into their tribes and ethnic groups. In short, Afghanistan was going to have to be completely rebuilt from the ground up.

Assignment

I began to get my life organized to leave since I would be starting pre-deployment training in the spring and had to make sure all was prepared in case I was killed, and my family would need to know what to do. I dropped out of school and went home to Wisconsin to see my family since I would not see them for a long time. Because I was not married or tied down in any way, the transition was easy for me, and having been to so many countries already it was not a big deal for me to drop everything and go. Since I had only left Egypt the summer before, I barely had enough time to get moved and accustomed to Florida before I had to leave again.

My classmates seemed baffled by my sudden departure. For them, it was unthinkable. None of them really thought about life outside of their daily bubbles, and I was kind of amazed that many of my friends asked me, "Afghanistan? We are still over there?" It surprised me that we could be involved in two simultaneous conflicts overseas, but for most people it was not a big thing for them. Life did not really change for those who did not serve or who were not directly affected by the conflicts.

I was assigned to the 492nd Civil Affairs Battalion (CA BN) in Arizona. It was a unit thrown together of officers and enlisted Soldiers from all over the country, mostly from Texas. We all assembled in the spring of 2005 in Phoenix and met our teams and started getting to know each other. It would be a long stint consisting of months of training and a full year in Afghanistan. Needless to say, we were a group of strangers that would need to come together as brothers and sisters really quickly since our lives depended on our cohesiveness. I was blessed with a great team of people, and we would later be referred to as the dream team that a lot of other guys had wished they were on. We certainly had our issues, but all in all it was a great group.

The Team

Our original team consisted of eight people, including myself. I will not name them in order to maintain their anonymity. However, two of the most senior members of our team were both expelled from our unit and sent elsewhere due to fighting with each other. It was all for the best, though. We had the most solid team that I could have asked for. Each one of us was ready for the mission. We were all team players and did not let petty personal issues get in the way of our work. Each person on the team brought individual talents and experience that made us unique.

Evenings after training were boring, so we often got together to watch movies and relax. One of our favorite movies was a comedy called "Tomcats." We watched that movie so many times that we decided our team should be nicknamed Tomcats. We even changed our call signs for radio calls to include the name. As the team commander, I was referred to as Tomcat 6. I will never forget the first time someone called me on the radio with a confused voice, "Ah, Tomcat 6???" It was pretty unusual, but we all needed a good laugh sometimes.

Training

After we all met in Phoenix, the entire battalion of the 492nd CA BN flew out to a small Army Reserve training base in California for pre-deployment training. With the Iraq War in full swing and the Afghanistan campaign mostly neglected, our training was laughable. Nearly every instructor conducted their training as though we were deploying to Iraq. We kept hearing from every instructor, "When you get to Iraq …," and we all groaned, "We are going to Afghanistan!!!" The instructors would mostly say, "Oh, well, I'm not sure about Afghanistan."

The training that was designed for Civil Affairs teams was equally pointless. The instructors would create scenarios designed to throw everything one might encounter on a typical Civil Affairs mission into one scenario. Many Civil Affairs missions dealt with meeting community officials out in rural areas, which could be extremely dangerous. The instructors set up scenarios where the team would drive to the meeting place, start a meeting for five minutes, get attacked, and then get ambushed all in a 10-minute span. That was the extent of Civil Affairs mission training. The whole goal was to push as many teams through the silly exercise as quickly as possible to check the box and say, "You Are Trained." Other mission scenarios were conducted, but they were poorly thought out and, again, were mostly based on Iraq issues that were very different from Afghanistan's.

Cultural training — something that was very vital for soldiers who had never been outside of the U.S., let alone in a completely alien environment such as Afghanistan — consisted of a one-hour briefing from an Afghan native. It was an eye-opening experience to see that so many Soldiers were not able to understand that people from other countries like Afghanistan grew up in a vastly different environment than they had. Afghans' culture, values, beliefs, and views of the world are quite different in many respects, and one cannot simply treat them as inferior because they have different ways of doing things. One crazy example was when during the culture briefing the instructor tried to explain a little about Islam to the auditorium of over 500 people. One Soldier raised his hand and asked, "Why don't we just convert them all to Christianity?" It seemed that the whole room gasped at the same time the instructor's jaw dropped to the floor. The instructor tried to explain how that was not possible and it could be awfully bad for him if he tried to convert Afghans to Christianity. One of my fellow team commanders turned to me and said, "I wonder what poor son of a bitch has that guy on his team?" I said that I thought that guy should be pulled from the deployment, as he could certainly endanger the mission. Our job was to work with the population and not piss them off by starting a religious fight.

After a few weeks in California, we all flew to Fort Bragg for our final training and deployment. It was a blessing for me since I had been stationed at Fort Bragg years before, and some of my friends in the 82nd Airborne and U.S. Special Forces units were still stationed there or had returned. It was great to see them again before heading out to Afghanistan. Despite the poor training, we were beginning to bond as a unit and were getting to know each other well. We had a few nights that were free to go out on the town. One of those nights a bunch of us decided to check out one of the many strip clubs near Fort Bragg. We piled 10 people in a giant Cadillac that one of the guys rented for the night (yes, two people fit in the trunk). We had a great time, and on the way back onto the base, the gate guard stopped us and wanted to search the car. When he opened the trunk to find two people in there he was a bit surprised. We told him, "Come on, man, we are headed to war in a couple days!" The guard laughed and told us to "go and have a good night." I thought that was pretty cool of him.

Arrival in Afghanistan

As we landed at Bagram Airfield in Afghanistan, things began to become a whole lot more real. At that time in June of 2005, the base was still pretty primitive, consisting of a lot of wooden huts and built-up aircraft hangars. It always seemed like mass confusion, trying to organize hundreds of people all trying to figure out what will happen next. Hundreds of us were corralled into a giant open tent with hundreds of small Army cots strewn all over the place in a complete mess. Each team, including my own, grabbed a bunch and organized ourselves into a small grouping. Each team was later assigned a particular province — the U.S. equivalent of a state — that it would be sent to the next week. My team was assigned to the Nangarhar Province in the east. We knew nothing about the place at the time, so we all huddled around a map looking at the terrain and trying to get oriented. We were told that the current team in Nangarhar would be coming to pick us up, and we would drive to the province with them. Each of the teams that we had been training with for the last few months would be heading off to their provinces, and we would not see many of them until we all came back together at the end of the year.

The team that we were replacing picked us up around noon on a hot June day. After giving us a quick convoy briefing, we all huddled into a few beat-up pickup trucks and old Humvees with no doors or even roofs. We all thought it was a bit strange that there were no armored vehicles, and some of the pickup trucks looked far from road worthy. But we were the new guys, so we just went with it, figuring all of our questions would be answered later.

The drive from Bagram Airfield to our base in the city of Jalalabad in the Nangahar Province was quite the experience. In 2005, the main roads were under construction, and the highway system consisted of two-lane roads that went through every village on the way. What would have been a three-hour drive on good roads took us about seven hours. The drive took us through mountain passes that were far from safe, with 1,000-foot drops and no real guardrails. Afghans are not exactly slow, careful drivers, either, even on those crazy mountain passes. But after several hours of white-knuckle mountain and off-road driving, we finally made it to Jalalabad, where we would spend the next year of our lives (and I would end up spending another six years more).

The Mountain Road to Jalalabad

Driving through the city was an eye-opening experience. The buildings were crumbling. Mud and cement walls lined the streets, as every property needed to be secured from the outside world. The roads were full of sewage, and garbage was strewn all over the place. Goats and dogs ran wild through the streets, picking at piles of trash for something to eat. Unsupervised children played in the streets and gave us a thumbs-up sign as we drove by, trying not to splash sewage on them from the giant puddles everywhere. It was clear from the beginning that the place needed a lot of help.

Nangarhar Province was a beautiful place. In general, it could be considered like a bowl with mountains all around its edges, where streams would cut through several small valleys and meet at the center in one large river that flowed into Pakistan, which bordered the province to the east. Jalalabad was the main urban center of the province and was where the majority of the population lived and worked. Jalalabad was one of the largest cities in Afghanistan, with a population of over 350,000. It was also the center of government for the Nangarhar Province and was the home of the governor and provincial council. The city of Jalalabad had one of the largest universities in the country and had a high percentage of educated people compared to the rest of Afghanistan. Nangarhar Province was made up of 22 districts, similar to counties in the United States. Each district had its own police force, district sub-governor, and district council of elders. Those groups held the power in the districts and became the groups that I dealt with often.

The Nangarhar PRT

Our Civil Affairs team was assigned to the Nangarhar Provincial Reconstruction Team, better known as the PRT. Every province had one of those PRTs that was tasked to work with the provincial government to help "reconstruct" the province. The PRT consisted of a military Civil Affairs component that was the lead team dealing with civilian issues related to the military occupation in that province, a U.S. State Department representative to be the U.S. chief civilian diplomat for the province, a United States Agency for International Development (USAID) officer who was in charge of overseeing U.S. humanitarian and reconstruction aid programs, and a U.S. military commander to overall be in charge of the unit. Ideally, those civilian and military components would work together as a cohesive team to help the Afghans rebuild both the infrastructure and institutions that could help Afghanistan become a stable country after 30 years of conflict. With the Afghan government still in a nascent stage, the PRTs ended up being almost a shadow government where citizens would come to ask for everything from drinking water wells and roads for their villages to resolution of conflicts between villages. In 2005, we stopped taking direct requests from villages and pushed citizens to lobby their own government, which by then had departments that could address those issues.

The Nangarhar PRT base was an old, abandoned Soviet boarding area for its pilots who flew missions out of the nearby Jalalabad Airfield. The airfield was taken over by the U.S. military and was occupied by a battalion of Marines that had an infantry battalion stationed there. The PRT base consisted of a dormitory building where we could house troops; an office building; a large drained pool with many bullet holes in it, which we were told was a site of executions by the Taliban; and a small building used as a dining hall. There was also a landing zone where helicopters could land and often did, day and night. The base housed our PRT teams and also had some other small units, like an intelligence cell, an aviation team, a psychological operations team, and a police training team. That hodgepodge of units worked their separate missions, and sometimes we teamed up to go to places around the province if we had compatible missions. Compared to other bases around Afghanistan, the Nangarhar PRT base was a decent place to be, with lush gardens and trees that were a nice change from the dusty, hot, and dry areas that most bases occupied.

Transition with Outgoing Team

As we settled into our new surroundings, we only had about a week to transition with the outgoing team before we were out on our own. The outgoing team did not have much of a plan for transition, and it was clear that there were some serious rifts between members of the PRT team. My counterpart commander, whom I was taking over for, was not very informative. The team that we took over for had spent the following year running around the province conducting random meetings with local elders, built a few schools and flood protection walls (floodwalls) on some waterways, and purchased two dozen police cars for local law enforcement. They said that the police had just started wearing their uniforms and that that was a triumph. Their expectations for the province could be wrapped up in one sentence that they used: "Just get them to stop shitting in the street!"

The poor attitude that they had toward their jobs infuriated me at first, but I suppose I had to put it in some context. They were probably exhausted from the year and more than ready to leave. I would have appreciated more information and a better handover experience, but after a while I was just happy to see them leave.

All we were left with was about 200 reports that documented their meetings. Those were of little use to an incoming team. As a Civil Affairs team commander I was interested in knowing things like who the main power players were throughout the province and what the state of infrastructure was and how projects were conducted, since I was in charge of our military's rebuilding efforts in the province, as well. In order to best know what to focus on over the next year, it would have been good to have some context on those things. We received no useful help. The outgoing commander rarely talked to me and answered questions using as few words as possible. The bottom line was that the guy was an unhelpful, unprofessional jerk, and I would later find out that everyone else felt that way about him, too. We did go on a couple of missions outside of the base to familiarize ourselves with the city and local communities. The outgoing team had chosen one village on the outskirts of the city of Jalalabad that was to be its adopted village. Team members brought gifts to the elders and stopped by to visit them on a regular basis.

Driving down dirt streets through Jalalabad and the outer districts in our beat-up pickup trucks and open-air Humvees with no doors or roofs was a strange thing. With the roads all in a state of disrepair, traffic was crazy and mostly just a mess of cars following no rules, often leading to traffic jams. We were very vulnerable to attack since we had no protection. Sitting in a traffic jam with no doors meant someone could just sit behind a wall near a major intersection and shoot at us like sitting ducks. Luckily, we did not have such bad luck early in the deployment. Within about two months we were given new armored trucks, fresh off of the assembly line. They ended up proving their worth quickly.

Civil Affairs Role

As Civil Affairs Soldiers it was our job to go out and deal with the civilian population daily. We went on missions throughout Nangarhar Province every day of the week except Friday, which is the Muslim holy day. We used that day to clean our equipment, play dominoes, watch movies, and rest for a day before starting the new week of missions. Our team quickly got into a groove, and we became a tight group. I was lucky to have such professional guys on my team who were very dedicated to the job and had no fear of going out on any mission. We all wanted to succeed and do our part to help Afghanistan improve. To differentiate us from other units, we wore baseball caps instead of helmets in the field and modified our body armor to be less bulky. It was easy to tell who we were when civilians saw us. I wore my St. Louis Cardinals hat on every mission. Although traditional Army units would scoff at our approach, we saw it as a way to be more approachable to civilians instead of looking like unapproachable robots full of body armor with eyes hiding behind dark sunglasses.

The Tomcats (I am second from the right)

Interpreters and PRT Local Staff

After we finished transitioning with the outgoing team, we assumed responsibility for all of the military-funded infrastructure projects in the province. Those included a couple of schools, some floodwalls on some rivers, and a couple of other small projects that were being completed. I received a new interpreter named Ahmad, right after arriving in Nangarhar, replacing an interpreter who decided to leave along with the outgoing team. Ahmad was an Afghan-American who was a truck driver in the U.S., and was a CAT I interpreter, meaning he was an American and had a secret clearance, so he was paid much better than the other locally hired interpreters at the PRT. Shortly after my team took over for the outgoing one, one of the local Afghan contractors, who was building a floodwall for us, came to the PRT and met with Ahmad. He handed my new interpreter $5,000 in cash and told him, "Here is your cut; tell the PRT engineer that I will have his cut next week." That contractor was building a $30,000 floodwall and was kicking back $10,000 to the interpreter and engineer for the Civil Affairs team. I think that there were even more kickbacks paid to the community elders and possibly others on the PRT team, as well. It made me wonder how much it actually cost to build the floodwall if at least 30 percent was already kicked back to just two individuals. The interpreter immediately brought the money to me and said, "I want no part of this."

But it was obvious that a pay-for-play strategy was being employed at the PRT, and that was no way to conduct business on my watch. I brought the interpreter and money to the PRT commander, and she was obviously pissed. I said that was probably the case with all of the projects that had been tendered by the PRT. I did not know how right I was.

Suddenly the same day I was called into the PRT commander's office, and the local police liaison, who lived at the PRT base, told us that one of our interpreters for the Civil Affairs team had been involved in a kickback scheme involving illegally harvested timber from nearby Kunar Province. They took the interpreter away and put him in the local Jalalabad city jail at the police station downtown. The interpreter would not even look at me. He had shame in his eyes, but also had a look like he had more to say but was afraid. It was clear that there were a lot of corrupt things going on at the Nangarhar PRT.

After everyone else had left her office, the commander turned to me and said, "Chris I want you to conduct an investigation and get to the bottom of what is happening with corruption in our local staff." I was just starting to get settled at the PRT and was already conducting an investigation of the entire local staff at the PRT. I started with the locally hired interpreters who worked for my Civil Affairs team. I interviewed one guy, and he simply said he did not know anything and denied all allegations of any wrongdoing on his part. I told him that I was going to get to the bottom of it all one way or another. That evening word had gotten out that I was investigating, and I began to get strange calls from local staff members. One of my interpreters called me in a state of panic. He said, "Sir, if anyone mentions something about a stereo, I had nothing to do with it!" I said, "Stereo? What the heck are you talking about?" He said, "Sir, if I get fired and have to go back to my village I will be killed since they all know I work with the U.S. military. Please sir, save my life!" I told him to tell me what was happening, and I would not fire him.

To make a long story short, it seemed that nearly every transaction made by the PRT had some sort of kickbacks and corruption involved with it. We soon found out that most of the local Afghan staff members were in on it to some degree. The problem was trying to prove it and then, of course, taking legal action against so many staff members in an unstable and dangerous place. The commander decided to basically have a blanket amnesty and then put processes in place to stop corruption in the future. I went down to the police station and freed our interpreter there, and told him that we were starting over, and no further issues would be tolerated from anyone. He did not say anything but "Thank you!"

Mission Strategy

Our strategy going into the year was to get to all 22 districts, assess the issues and problems there, forge relationships with the elders and local population, and see where our interventions could help. We also planned to help create some synergy between the districts and the provincial government directors, such as the director of education and director of rural development. That way the communities would start going to their government officers for help instead of coming to us to ask for help. Our thoughts were that the sooner people would start working with their own government the sooner they would start trusting their own government. We had also planned to create some knowledge management so that the things we learned during the year would be captured and useful for the next teams that came after us. As we began our daily missions out to the districts, we quickly found that there was not a single paved road in the whole province, and each dirt road was in a horrible state of disrepair. A trip that would take 30 minutes in the U.S., took hours on those roads.

The Round Robin Tour

We began our year by meeting all of the leaders of the Nangarhar Province and conducting missions to every district in the province. Some of the districts were close to our base near the capital of Jalalabad, and some were at least a day's drive due to the horrible road conditions that forced us to drive at about 20 mph maximum in most areas. Our objective of each mission was to meet the district sub-governors and police chiefs of each district; assess the area for security, infrastructure, and stability; and see where we might be able to help them or work together to ensure the areas stayed stable. Most of our meetings were conducted under trees, in small tents, or in rundown buildings that were barely standing. Years later each district would receive a district administration building, a police station, and other buildings, but that was 2005, and there was little infrastructure.

One district that we had visited several times was Sherzad District. It was a pretty dangerous area, and the district administration and police station occupied a walled-in, rundown building with no windows and a leaking roof, that looked like a tornado had hit it. We always camped overnight there with the police who offered to let us stay in the building, but we were happy to sleep out under the stars where a building would not fall on us. The most striking feature of the compound was the 10-foot-high marijuana bush in the middle of the driveway. It appeared that the police were happy to partake in smoking their weed, and out in that area it may have been the best way to remain calm in such a dangerous place.

Weed at the Police Station

Achin Visit

One of the first districts we visited was the Achin District. That district borders Pakistan and was well known for its opium poppy cultivation, drug smuggling through the mountain passes into Pakistan, and bad guys coming from Pakistan across the border into Afghanistan using the same mountain passes. Achin was the sight of the 2017 U.S. bombing campaign against ISIS where the "Mother of All Bombs" was dropped, creating a massive explosion in the Achin border region. That visit to Achin was pretty eye opening for a new person who just arrived in Afghanistan. We pulled up to the district headquarters, which consisted of a small area with some chairs under a tree where the district sub-governor and police chief conducted meetings. I got out of the Humvee and took off all of my gear and weapons. I never conducted meetings with body armor and weapons showing. Those guys were our allies in that fight, so why treat them like they were adversaries. That being said, I always had my pistol stuck in my belt in the back, covered by my uniform top just in case.

Our meeting began with shaking hands and introducing ourselves through my interpreter. Our two field interpreters were part of the team in every way. They took more risk than we did, and they earned our respect and trust quickly. The sub-governor invited us into the tent and offered us some green tea, which was practically a must-drink at every meeting. Since I had attended hundreds of meetings in the field throughout my time in Afghanistan I have drunk hundreds of gallons of green tea.

I began by asking the sub-governor about the security situation and opium poppy cultivation in the area. He told me that security was improving but there were some bad actors that had come in from Pakistan when the mountain passes were open in the summer and the snow was melted. He told me that poppy cultivation was down since there was an agreement with the government to stop growing poppies in exchange for infrastructure projects. That was a lie; there was poppy grown in his area that year, but it was significantly less than had been grown normally. Achin was known as a major heroin processing area, as well as for opium poppy growing. The refined heroin or raw opium was then smuggled into Pakistan and distributed throughout the world.

I told the sub-governor and police chief that I had been told recently that we had the money to build girls' schools if they needed them. The sub-governor began to laugh. He said, "We don't really need the girls to be educated. They are just going to be taking care of children or sold off to repay debts." I was taken by surprise with that answer. Even though I knew it happened, to have a community leader just come out and nonchalantly say that little girls should stay dumb and that they can be traded for debt like a commodity was crazy. It was even stranger that he was laughing about it. That sub-governor was quite old and seemed a little past his prime. He ended up being replaced not long after our meeting and was never seen in leadership positions again. Hopefully he retired, as he was a poor example of leadership. Most of our other 21 district trips went better. Meetings were often held under a tree in a garden or in a rundown building that the government took over. However, by the end of 2006 nearly every district had a new district administration building constructed so there would be no more meetings under trees.

Meeting District Sub-Governors Under a Tree

The First IED

Building infrastructure projects with the local communities is one of the important roles of a Civil Affairs team. Each project would be celebrated with an opening ceremony once the project was completed. In August of 2005, our team finished construction of a school expansion in the extremely dangerous district of Pacir Wa Agam. This was the district containing the Tora Bora complex where Bin Laden had escaped from in 2001, and the place was known to have a lot of Taliban/Al Qaida sympathizers. Our team headed down to the district center where the school was located. The road on the way there was a horrible dirt road with no culverts, where irrigation and drainage ditches could cross under the road. Therefore, little streams of water crossed over the roads causing kind of an inverted speed bump that would jar the trucks as they went across. Those streams also covered up any possible digging into the road. If an insurgent wanted to place a bomb in the road, it was the perfect place to put it to avoid detection.

As we arrived at the school, the whole community greeted us. District leaders gave speeches, children sang songs and danced for us in celebration, and the whole place was in a cheery mood. One police officer who had met me on the long mission that we had done with the Special Forces team the prior week saw me and gave me a big hug and asked me to sit with him at the celebration. He said he needed to talk to me after the festivities. At the end of the celebration, we cut a ribbon to officially open the school, and members of the local population were allowed to ask us questions and speak to us directly. The elders cried that more projects were needed and that we should be doing more. They said we were safe there and the community would guarantee our security. There was rightly a lot of frustration and impatience with the slow pace of infrastructure development in those rural districts, and people were starting to get frustrated. I told them we would be back to work with them on new project ideas as long as they took care of security.

As we prepared to leave the area, my police officer friend pulled me to the side and said, "Chris I know where there are some Al Qaida agents who are living in a compound not far from here." He asked me to relay this message to the Special Forces team commander so that we could get a plan together to take them out. I told him I would get in touch with the Special Forces team commander right away. He also said, "Make sure you do not take the same way home." I said, "Okay, thanks brother, I will contact you soon." As we pulled away from the school we were only about 100 yards away when suddenly the truck in front of me exploded before my eyes. The hood of the damaged truck flew up and landed right in front of our car. It really did feel like time slowed down. As the commander of the team I said the only thing I could, "Holy shit!" The explosion seemed so big that I was sure that everyone in the truck was injured or killed. I quickly ordered the team to form a security perimeter, not knowing if a follow-on attack was coming. Being a certified EMT, as well, I grabbed the medical bag and jumped out of the truck to the smoldering Humvee. As I approached the truck the doors swung open, and smoke poured out of it. I yelled, "Are you guys okay? Are you guys okay?" Amazingly all of the guys exited the vehicle completely unharmed. I was shocked.

The whole community gathered on hills surrounding us and watched as we gathered ourselves together. Suddenly a man with a metal box jumped up in the middle of a field near the bomb site and started running. The Afghan police who traveled with us started shouting and shooting at the guy. Apparently we had found the trigger-man, as that was a remote-controlled IED. As the man ran everyone opened fire on him, and he stopped and hit the ground. I thought he had been hit, but he jumped right back up and started running again. We started shooting at him again. He was about 300 yards away from us, but we were obviously bad shots. It really is different shooting at a moving target that far away versus a paper target. It was the first and only time I shot at anyone in my life. The man hit the ground, and we wanted to take him alive. The police, my team sergeant, and I were all in a race to capture him. As I ran I forgot that I was wearing a couple dozen pounds of extra stuff. As I leaped down a four-foot ledge my knee gave out, and I fell flat on my face, rifle flying off. My team sergeant ran right past me, laughing as he went by. It was pretty embarrassing. In the end, the police tackled the guy and flex cuffed him. We walked him over to the road and sat him down. I called the base and explained what had happened. A team was dispatched to come recover the vehicle. In the meantime, I sat down on the ground, and the sub-governor and police chief came and sat next to me. I asked, "So how is that security guarantee going?" The sub-governor was clearly embarrassed and said, "Well, sometimes the bad guys come." He brought some food and drinks for us, and we talked for several hours. I told him that we would not be doing any more projects for their district if that was their idea of security. The U.S. Special Forces team showed up a couple of hours later and took custody of the suspect that we had caught. Once the recovery team got there, we hitched up the truck and headed back to the base. It was a long, painful day. I got back to my room, put my head in my hands, and thanked God we had all made it. It turned out that the bomb was dug a little too far down into the road, and it exploded under the engine compartment instead of the passenger compartment. The armor held up well, and I was always thankful for armored trucks after that.

The Marines

Nangarhar Province had a company of Marines that was stationed to protect against any insurgent threats in the area. They were good guys, but quite rambunctious and always looking for a fight even where none existed. They were taught to trust no one and be prepared to kill anything not dressed like them. Needless to say, they had a hard time getting along with the local population and often made enemies with their poor behavior toward Afghans. Since we had a small team, we often needed some extra guys to serve as drivers, medics, communications guys for long missions, or to man the gun turrets in the Humvees. Some of the Marines would help fill those roles. On one particular mission, a Marine sergeant was manning a gun turret above me in my Humvee. Due to the awful road conditions in the city of Jalalabad we were stuck in a nasty traffic jam at a major intersection. Every vehicle was stuck, and there was nothing we could do about it until things started freeing up in front of us.

Suddenly I started seeing water bottles bouncing off of cars around us. As the mission commander I got on the radio and asked all personnel to tell me if they were seeing that, too. The Marine gunner above me replied, "Yes, sir, it was me. I am trying to get the cars to move out of the way!" He kept throwing those full water bottles, and one even looked like it dented a car next to ours. The drivers, of course, looked pissed and like they wanted to kill someone. I saw that and called up to the gunner throwing the bottles, "Are you kidding me? You throw another bottle at these cars, and I will throw you out to them." A pause went over the radio, and then the gunner said, "Understood, Sir!" I got out of my Humvee and walked around the truck, gesturing to the Afghans driving the cars. I pointed at the guy who threw the bottles, and then shook my head and put my hand on my heart in a show of apology. The Afghan guys smiled and waved, as if to say thanks for showing respect for us. It only takes one minute to make an enemy, and that kind of stupid act is a perfect way to turn people against you.

During another mission to the Ghosta District to visit the sub-governor and police chief, one of the Marine lieutenants asked if he could tag along and do a patrol around the area while we conducted our meeting with the sub-governor. It was a long, dangerous trip to Ghosta so I thought it would be a great idea to have a platoon of Marines with us just in case things went badly. We arrived at the district center, and one of the drivers fell ill from heat exhaustion. He fainted, and some of the guys carried him to the truck and pumped him full of air conditioning and water. It was so hot in Nangarhar, and wearing 30 pounds of equipment and weaponry was an easy way to become a heat casualty if you did not drink plenty of water and electrolytes.

As usual, the other team members and I took off all of our body armor and weapons and went into the tent with just our pistols hidden. The sub-governor and police chief greeted us and brought out more tea and treats for us. We talked about the issues in the district and got to know them and their backgrounds a bit. Suddenly, a young Marine poked his head into the tent and said, "Sir, the lieutenant wanted to know if he can come in and join the meeting." I said, "Sure, that would be great." The Marine lieutenant and two of his sergeants quickly came into the tent with full battle gear and rifles held as though they were ready to fight. The sub-governor had a grin on his face and kind of chuckled at the sight of those guys. I jumped up in front of them and pushed them out of the tent. I pulled the lieutenant to the side and said, "What the hell are you doing coming in there like that?" The young lieutenant said, "What? I want to intimidate him." I wondered why in the heck would he want to intimidate his ally. What have they been teaching those guys? I told him, "This sub-governor was a former Mujahedeen commander who fought the Soviets for years. You really think he is going to be intimidated by a 23-year-old kid? Take off your gear, and come in quietly and listen for a while, and I will introduce you."

The lieutenant and his guys came in quietly a few minutes later. I introduced him to the sub-governor and asked if the lieutenant wanted to ask anything. The lieutenant said, "I just wanted to meet you and let you know that I'm in charge of security around here." I could not help but grin a little as the police chief said to the sub-governor, "I thought I was in charge of security?" in a half joking, condescending way. Needless to say, the meeting did not go very well. When we got back to the base, I popped over to the company commander of all of those Marine lieutenants and told him about his guys' behavior. I said that I know the guys are hard-charging Marines, and are doing their best and have good intentions, but they need to tone it down, and know the difference between friends and enemies. We both had a good laugh about it, and he said he would talk to his "knuckleheads." They did end up softening up a bit over the year.

Although I gave the Marines a hard time for their belligerent behavior, it was in their training and DNA to be seen as tough and aggressive. For instance, there was a list of "rules" painted on the wall in front of a urinal in the bathroom at the base. One of the rules was a quote from Marine General "Mad Dog" Mattis, "Be polite, be professional, but have a plan to kill everybody you meet!" With that kind of mentality ingrained into each Marine, it is easy to stop seeing local Afghans as regular people and instead seeing everyone as enemies. That mentality may be useful in a fight or in a regular war against uniformed enemies, but it is certainly not useful when you are occupying someone else's country and need to make alliances with the local population in order to succeed. In fairness, not every Marine in Afghanistan acted that way. Many of the Marines we worked with on a daily basis understood the mission and were very professional toward the Afghans.

Humanitarian Aid to Returnee Camps

Another part of the Civil Affairs role was monitoring the two large returnee camps that were located near Jalalabad. Those camps were called Tangi Behsud and Sheikh Mesri. Although we mistakenly called them refugee camps, they were really "returnee" camps. A refugee is someone fleeing their country and staying in a different country. Those camps were filled with Afghans who had fled the country years ago but had returned to Afghanistan with nowhere to go. Pakistan had hosted Afghans in refugee camps for decades in their country and was starting to close those camps and send Afghans back home. That caused a bit of a crisis since those people had no home to go back to. The masses of returnees began settling on dry pieces of land outside of the city of Jalalabad that became the Tangi Behsud and Sheikh Mesri returnee camps.

The makeshift camps in 2005 consisted of mostly handmade tents, constructed of anything the people could get their hands on. There was no clean source of water, so people were drinking out of a nearby irrigation canal that they shared with animals. It was hard to imagine drinking from water that was tainted with animal and human waste, as well as agriculture runoff. The people were desperate and needed help. The U.N. High Commissioner for Refugees was in charge of helping those people, but progress was slow. We took it upon ourselves to bring whatever supplies we were given to try and help ease the suffering. We brought tarps for building shelters, blankets, food, little cookstoves, and radios. There was never enough to go around as the camps got bigger and bigger.

Unloading Supplies at a Refugee Camp

Things improved for those camps over the years. Wells were dug, shelters were provided, schools were created, roads were built, and eventually the government gave out plots of land to the returnees. The camp at Sheikh Mesri eventually became a real town, and people began to build actual houses. I remember one old man I had met there who was so happy to have a plot of land because his whole life he had never had a place to call his own. He came up to me with tears in his eyes and hugged me. It was hard to control my emotions seeing him. I think that helped solidify the sympathy I had for the people of Afghanistan who had been through so much pain for decades.

Ferry Across the River

There was one district called Lal Pur that is directly on the border with Pakistan. There are two ways to get to the district from Jalalabad: drive all the way around the Kabul River and take a bridge and drive up to five hours to get there, or take the world's most bizarre ferryboat and shave off a couple of hours of driving. We decided to go with the ferryboat to save time. Our armored Humvees at the time weighed a few tons and were not your typical vehicle to cross on the ferry. Our interpreters who had crossed before ensured us that it would be safe. As we pulled up to the ferry-docking site, we saw that the ferryboat was nothing but a couple of canoe-like boats strapped together with an old Air Force pallet nailed to them to create a space for a car to sit on. There was a rope strewn across the river from one side to the other that guided the boat, and the current of the river provided the propulsion. It was a pretty genius setup that saved hours of driving for those brave enough to use the ferry. I thought that it might be a bit sketchy and was thinking of calling it off when a large dump truck suddenly pulled up onto the ferryboat. I thought that if it would hold that thing then we would be good. In just a couple of minutes, the truck was swooped away across the river and safely drove off on the other side. We then proceeded to get our three Humvees across the river and carried out the rest of our mission. Looking back, it was such a risky move that I wonder how I would have explained it if one of our Humvees was lost in the river with millions of dollars of equipment on board. I think that meeting would have been rather harsh.

Tora Bora Mission

About halfway through our tour we were told that my team would spearhead a mission to Tora Bora as part of an annual show of force to remind the local population that we were there. For those who do not know or forgot, Tora Bora was the mountain pass area full of tunnels and cliffs from where Osama Bin Laden escaped during the U.S. attack in 2001. It was the last time anyone saw Bin Laden until the night of his death. The Tora Bora area is in the Pacir Wa Agam District, which is where we were hit by our first IED after the opening of the school. Our staging area for the mission was the same school building that we were opening that day. As we drove over the same spot where the bomb had disabled our vehicle a couple months prior, my jaw clenched but relaxed as we rolled safely over the stream. We slept in the school that night, and in the morning I organized the team to go into the mountain pass.

The team consisted of my Civil Affairs team, one platoon of Marines, and one platoon of the Afghan National Army. As the highest ranking person in the group I assumed command of the mission but delegated convoy command duties to the Marine lieutenant, since he and his Afghan Army cohort made up the bulk of the group, and they obviously had more direct action training than I did. It was kind of nice to be able to be on a tactical mission where I did not have to worry about all of the logistics and leadership and could relax a little. It was short lived, however, since the Marine lieutenant got lost on the way, and we ended up having to backtrack a couple of times. I could not fault him much, though, as it was an area with very few marked roads, and it was tricky to find the right trail to take us into the mountain pass.

Once we found the right trail, it took us to a one-lane track that led us into the mountains on the most dangerous "road" I have ever been on. The road was barely wide enough for one Humvee to fit, and if another car had come the opposite way I had no idea how we could have passed. Luckily, no vehicles came the other way, since hardly anyone lives out there. The passenger side of my Humvee was so close to the edge that I could not see the road surface outside of my window. All I could see was a 1,000-foot drop to the bottom of the mountain. I must admit I was scared shitless but could not show my fear to the rest of the team members. I was their commander after all, so what kind of example would that set. Instead I told the driver, who was a Marine police sergeant, that if he needed to he should scrape the mountainside with his side of the Humvee to avoid getting too close to the edge. He sensed my apprehension and professionally said, "Don't worry, Sir, I have driven in a lot of worse spots than this. You are in good hands, Sir." He was right; he drove like a pro, and we all made it safely in and out of the pass without incident.

The road we were on through the mountains suddenly came to an end at a mountain stream with cliffs on either side. The "road" now consisted of just driving up a trickling stream like some kind of crazy rock-crawling competition. We were only 3 miles from our intended objective, but we were never going to make it before nightfall. We decided to bed down next to the streambed in the only flat place in the area, next to a small cluster of houses that had small plots of land irrigated by canals off of the mountain stream.

Since U.S. and Afghan troops rarely came to that area, it was a wild spectacle for the local people. Everyone came out of their homes to see what was going on. With no electricity or television in the area, our excursion into their lives was the most exciting thing to happen to them all year. Most people came out and sat on rocks in the stream and watched us all day and night. As a gesture of goodwill, my team gave out blankets and other provisions to the villagers, which they happily accepted. I talked to the head of the village, and he welcomed us and asked if there was anything they could do for us. I said that we could use some firewood. It was February in the mountains, and it was starting to get cold. Very quickly donkeys started popping out of the woods with bundles of firewood. We paid the villagers well for their service, and they just kept it coming. An old man came to me with a turkey and asked if I would like to buy it. I said no thank you, but we invited him to sit with us and talk for a while.

Our team set up our cots and provisions around a nice fire and talked with some of the local people. The Marines had created a security perimeter with the Afghan Army component. The leader of the village told us that we were welcome and would be safe there. I saw some local villagers keeping watch on the top of the cliffs. I felt that we were secure there regardless of our horrible tactical position in a valley surrounded by cliffs. As our team laughed and joked with the locals around a raging fire, cooking hot dogs and other stuff, the Marines huddled around their vehicles cold and unhappy, looking at us with jealousy while they burned tiny 1-foot piles of their trash in an attempt to stay hidden in the dark.

The Marine lieutenant platoon leader came over to me and said, "Sir, I'm not sure your fire is the most tactical thing to be doing right now." I chuckled, "Take a seat lieutenant." He came and sat down, and I said, "First of all, do you really think us being here is a mystery to the bad guys? Everyone knows we are here and probably knew we were coming before we even got here. Second, do you see those guys sitting on the cliffs with AK-47s? They are the local villagers keeping watch over us. Third, the biggest reason they are taking care of us is because we are buying a bunch of firewood and food from them at very generous prices. This is a windfall for them. The best thing you can do is go buy a bunch of firewood from these guys at $20 a donkey load, and they will love you forever. Keep your perimeter security up, of course, but make sure the guys get rested 'cause it is going to be a long day tomorrow." The look on the lieutenant's face was priceless. It was a scenario that was so outside of the type of thinking that was beaten into him for years during his Marine training. After a minute of blank staring, he shrugged his shoulders and said, "Okay, I get it." Soon the whole valley was filled with campfires and mingling with the locals. The night passed without incident, and we were all rested for the next day's activities.

Resting Between Missions in Tora Bora

The next day we were focused on getting to the objective village in the old Tora Bora stronghold. The trail up the streambed was amazing, and we put our new armored Humvees to the test. The stream cut a canyon through the mountains only about 50 feet wide in most places and sometimes as narrow as 10 feet. The stream was littered with boulders the size of our trucks, and the small track we had to follow was only passable with 4x4s. Those mountain areas contained some of the most beautiful white marble you would ever see. Many of the massive boulders we traversed were actually giant pieces of white marble. If harvested, those boulders would be worth tens of thousands of dollars. During our drive through the mountains, the Air Force dropped some humanitarian supplies for the villages by parachute, but they missed the tight valley by hundreds of yards, and the supplies landed up in the mountains. Some of the local people helped us track down the supplies, and we paid them to bring the stuff down from the mountains. They thankfully helped. One kid said he did not need to be paid, he just wanted to keep the parachute. I told him to take it and have a great time. He said it would be great to waterproof his roof with. Sounded pretty ingenious to me.

Driving Up the Streambed Next to Donkeys Hauling Wood

After hours of rock climbing driving up the mountain stream, we finally reached our destination village. It was a completely secluded village out of touch with the rest of the country. It had amazing terraced farm fields fed by an intricate irrigation canal system and a small micro-hydroelectric generator that ran off of falling water from the stream like an old water wheel, but it was in a state of complete disrepair. There was a school, clinic, and floodwall built by my team's predecessors years before. The villagers greeted us and welcomed us to the village. They set out a spread of food for us, and we ate with them and talked and got to know them. By the end of the meal, we were clapping along to songs as they played drums and sang. It was a lot of fun, and we made some good headway with them.

We then went out to a large open area in the stream, and I gave a speech to hundreds of local people who came out to see us. I told them about our goal to work with them to ensure security and humanitarian assistance along with the government. The sub-governor of the district and police chief showed up later that day, as well, and we all showed a united front of support for that secluded area. The villagers said it was the first time that the police chief and sub-governor had visited, and they were very appreciative. We gave out all of the humanitarian aid we had gotten from the Air Force airdrop that we had collected earlier in the day. After hours of visiting and listening to the concerns of the local people, we gathered ourselves together and headed back to base. It took us several hours to get back, but it was a bit quicker going down the mountain than it had been going up.

Talking to the Villagers in Tora Bora

Camels Smuggling Goods Back into Pakistan

One of the last district engagement missions was to the Dur Baba District, which was right on the Afghanistan-Pakistan border and was sparsely populated. There were only a few mixed villages spread out in the small valleys coming out of the dry mountains that created the border. As we traversed the nasty dirt road toward the district center we noticed that heading into the mountain passes from Afghanistan to Pakistan were several caravans of camels carrying various strange items — everything from car tires to mattresses. It seemed so crazy to us since the main highway from Afghanistan to Pakistan was only a couple of miles away. A simple truck would have been better and more efficient than strapping items to camels to carry across mountain passes into Pakistan. There was a very interesting trading strategy employed there.

The deep-water shipping Port of Karachi in southern Pakistan brought in all goods for Afghanistan since Afghanistan is landlocked and has no port of its own. In order to avoid Pakistani import taxes, importers would bring goods in through Karachi and mark them for export to Afghanistan, which had low import taxes. Trucks would pull off of the road near the border of the Dur Baba District and offload their goods to camels, which would then bring them illegally through the mountain passes back into Pakistan. What a painful process just to avoid Pakistani import taxes! The problem with that approach, besides loss of revenue to the Pakistani government, was that it encouraged illegal activities across the border. Keeping the smuggling routes open assisted in smuggling opium and heroin out, and insurgents and weapons into Afghanistan. It was an open secret that community leaders and government officials had interest in those illegal activities, so no action was really taken to stop them.

"Team America, Fuck Yeah!"

One team of Soldiers that often went with us on missions was the psychological operations (PSYOPS) team. It was a group that also dealt with the local population in order to influence their ideas about us. Their campaign was not very well thought through, and there did not seem be an actual PSYOPS strategy, at the provincial level anyway. So, the team would go out with us on missions and talk to local people while we conducted meetings with community leaders. The PSYOPS guys had huge loudspeakers on their truck for broadcasting messages to the population, but they never actually used it. The only thing they used it for was to blast the "Team America" movie soundtrack as we rolled out of the gate into the city. It was crazy to hear "Team America, Fuck Yeah!" blasted down the street. As funny as I thought it was, I had the team shut off the speakers once we reached the front gate, as I highly doubted the local population would have appreciated the song.

Bridge IED

Around October we had a mission down to the governor's compound to meet with the director of education, who was working with us to develop plans for school construction. Our meeting was short, and there was plenty of time left in the day to conduct a follow-on mission. I decided we would go and check out the Construction Trades Training Center (CTTC) that we were building in conjunction with USAID. It was a great project that ended up being very successful in the future, and I wanted to ensure everything was going okay. We needed to head just south of the city of Jalalabad and go over the main irrigation canal that fed most of the farms in the central Nangarhar Province.

There was a small bridge that we needed to traverse to get over the canal. As we crossed the bridge an explosion came from my right rear side. The blast hit my truck and the one behind me. Amazingly I did not even feel shocked or scared at all; just pissed. I yelled out, "Damn it!" All three of our trucks moved forward about 100 yards to the top of the bridge and checked that everyone was okay. The blast had knocked out my turret gunner above me, but he was all right, with just a scratch. The gunner in the truck behind us was singed a little, but everyone else was fine. It turned out that the blast was from a remote-controlled bomb strapped to a bicycle that was leaned up against the side of the bridge. The main concussion of the blast actually went between our two Humvees causing little damage to each of them.

An Afghan family that happened to be driving by in a little golf cart-like tuk-tuk was not so lucky. The family took the brunt of the blast, and the crowd had quickly gathered them up and rushed them to the hospital. We saw the remains of the destroyed tuk-tuk with shrapnel and blood on it. We did not know what happened to the family, but I was told later that at least two were killed. A young boy walking home from school was also killed. It is amazing sometimes what a decision like changing a mission can have on lives. Although it was not my fault, I always felt guilty about the deaths of those hit by that IED. It turns out that IED was most likely meant for another U.S. convoy that was going to be coming down that road on a planned mission south of Jalalabad in the Chaparhar District. Our driving by due to my change in mission ended up being a good target of opportunity.

Briefings to Generals and Congress Members

Since the Nangarhar PRT was relatively secure in the city of Jalalabad, and we were only a short helicopter ride from Kabul or Bagram Airfield, we became the place that all congressmen, ambassadors, and generals came for their site visits. During my year at the Nangarhar PRT, we conducted briefings for two four-star generals, one ambassador visit, and five congress members. It was always the same briefing and tour. We called it the "dog and pony show." It consisted of telling them that everything was great, the bad guys were on the run, our humanitarian and infrastructure programs were solving a whole bunch of social problems, and we were working great with the government. Of course, it was all a show. In effect, the Taliban and other insurgents were regrouping, our humanitarian aid and rebuilding programs were vastly underfunded and unorganized for what was needed, and the massive amount of government corruption and incompetence was causing the local population to become frustrated with the relatively new government. At the time, we were pretty naïve about the situation we were in. We may have thought we were doing great but just had no idea what was really happening out in the rural areas.

Friends Lost

Although my team and I were lucky enough to not have any injuries or deaths, other friends of ours were not so lucky. Of all of the hundreds of Civil Affairs Soldiers who deployed with us to Afghanistan that year, we lost three men. One of the lieutenant colonels, who led one of the PRTs in southern Afghanistan, died of natural causes only about a week into the deployment. I did not know him well, but he was always a good man around me, and he was well loved by the entire unit. When he died there were many teary eyes. The base he was in charge of was later named after him permanently. Another one of the guys was killed by an IED while walking outside of his vehicle. I did know him, and he was also just an all-around good guy and great Soldier.

The third man we lost was a little closer to my team. The Civil Affairs team from the Kunar Province came down from its base only a couple of hours away to pick someone up at our airfield. Their team came by our base to have lunch and hang out with us for a while. It was great to see them, as we had not seen them since the start of the deployment to Afghanistan. We laughed and joked and enjoyed lunch together. When we said goodbye, they headed back to their base, while our team got prepared to go over to the airfield to pick up some provisions. Their team went right, and our team went left out of our base. As we pulled into the Jalalabad Airfield a few minutes away there was a lot of traffic on the radio talking about an IED strike. It turned out that the team we had just had lunch with was hit, and one of our friends was killed in the blast. It was so strange thinking that someone I had just talked to and said, "We'll see you guys soon," was suddenly gone, and we would never see him again. I thought about his wife and kids, and how their lives were destroyed in the blink of an eye.

Darai Nur

In October, I was invited to a meeting in the Darai Nur District of Nangarhar, hosted by the United Nations. That district was quite different from the others in Nangarhar, as it was the home of the Pashai tribe. That area had villages that were cut off from the rest of Afghanistan and often kept to themselves politically and culturally. It was a beautiful mountain area that I had grown to love over my years in Afghanistan. The people in the area were notorious for having more Western-looking features, like light skin, light eyes, and even blonde hair. While I had heard several explanations for that, the reason the locals give is that the peoples are the offspring of Alexander the Great's army that ruled the area over 2,000 years ago. Their isolation from the rest of the world kept their genes from mixing with the Mongols, Mughals, Pashtuns, and other ethnic groups that dominate the area. Regardless of the reasons, it is an interesting story and anomaly in Afghanistan.

The meeting consisted of several aid groups and local community leaders from the Darai Nur District. One man, in particular, dominated the conversation. His name was Yasir Khan. He was a community leader from the northern part of the district, and it seemed that he was the unofficial spokesperson for the district, since everyone shut up and listened the moment he spoke. He was a blonde-haired, light-eyed man with light skin and facial features more like mine than any Afghan. His speech was a fiery one. He yelled about how Darai Nur had been very peaceful and cooperative with the government and stopped growing poppy, yet had been neglected with very little humanitarian aid or infrastructure projects to help their economy. He was not wrong. Darai Nur had been a very cooperative district and very little was done to help them. The district was in a remote area away from Jalalabad, and the roads to get there were horrible, causing a one-hour drive to take at least two.

Yasir Giving His Speech

Yasir looked at me several times during his long scolding of the international community. I was starting to learn how things worked around there with negotiations. Those kinds of public roasts were a way to shame people into doing more projects for them. As Yasir was done with his speech, he sat down still looking at me. We were in a stare-down contest for at least a minute when I let out a grin. Yasir then grinned too; he knew I understood his game. When the meeting was over, Yasir and I went off to the side and had our own meeting. He gestured to one of the younger Afghans, who then ran and gathered some tea and sweets for us. After the standard pleasantries, Yasir told me about Darai Nur's lack of roads, irrigation systems, schools, clinics, power, and virtually any economic development. He was a smart guy who really understood his area and honestly wanted to help his people. He invited me to visit his house for lunch in the future, so we could discuss it further.

Soon after that meeting, I took the team to Yasir's house in Darai Nur. It was the first time I went to someone's personal home. We sat on a dirt terrace in his yard away from the main house where the women were. The women were never shown outside of the house. Yasir's sons served us tea, vegetables, lamb, and potatoes. The scene was beautiful on the terrace, with lush fruit trees and a little irrigation stream running through the yard. I asked where I could use the bathroom before lunch. Yasir told me to just go on the other side of the terrace. There was just a ledge with trees around it with little turds lying all over the ground. I guess the idea was to just squat and let it fly. Over the years I would get used to it.

Lunch was delicious, with the freshest vegetables and fruits I had ever tasted. Yasir gave us an overview of Darai Nur and told us how the insurgents operated through the district; what routes they took; and offered to call us if he saw any nefarious characters, which he later did. He mentioned that the biggest problems in the district were the road system and getting power. He showed us a place in his backyard where he wanted to build a little micro-hydroelectric generator that would run off the falling water coming down the mountain through his backyard. He said that if we worked with him we could do it at cost, saving a ton of money. I thought that sounded like a good idea. So, we worked with Yasir to build the system. The total cost to us was only $10,000, and I looked at it as a good pilot project that could be replicated throughout the province. Yasir made good on his promise and ran power lines all over the village, providing light to nearly everyone at night. Most people paid him the equivalent of a dollar a month if they could afford it, just to keep up maintenance on the system. I knew Yasir loved to use the project to raise his standing in the community, but I did not care. The guy obviously deserved it for the work he was doing for them. Yasir and I became even closer friends in later years, and he would help me do even more amazing things for Darai Nur.

The drive home was a bit faster going down the mountain. The road was only wide enough to fit one vehicle. If another car came from the other direction, one would have to pull off to the side and wait. Ordinarily cars would get out of the way of our very wide Humvees. However, on the way down a car tried to come the other way and our mirrors clashed, breaking off the car's mirror. The rule we were told was to just keep driving back to the base, and the person could come and make a claim at the PRT later. I know the rule was meant to protect us from a conflict in the field, but I was more concerned about making an enemy in the place where we just had started a great relationship.

I told the driver to pull over, and I exited the vehicle. The other driver got out and approached me sternly. Talking through my interpreter, I apologized for hitting him and offered him a $20 bill from my pocket. The man smiled and thanked me and asked if we wanted to come to his house up the road for lunch. I politely declined, as we had just had lunch at Yasir's house. He thanked me for stopping and happily went on his way. I thought about that encounter often and wonder how he would have felt if we had just driven away after hitting his car. I doubt he would have had good feelings toward the U.S. military. Instead we made a friend.

Bin Laden's House/Pens for Peace

Just south of Jalalabad was one of Osama Bin Laden's old houses. The house had been bombed by U.S. Tomahawk missiles back in 1998 after Al Qaeda's bombing of the U.S. embassies in Kenya and Tanzania. President Clinton ordered the bombing of several Al Qaeda locations, hoping to hit Bin Laden but without luck. It was a rite of passage to stop by and hang American flags on the remaining walls of the destroyed house. We then would give the flags out to people at home or keep them for ourselves as great souvenirs. Of course, as men we had to take the opportunity to pee on the house, as well. I was able to spell out NYC for New York City on the wall of his former house. Sure, it was pretty immature, but it gave us a great feeling for a day to enact a little American childish revenge.

Osama Bin Laden's Old House

From the beginning of our deployment, everywhere we went we were inundated by children chasing after us, mostly cheering and waving and giving us a strange sign with their hands. When I was new to the country I had no idea what they were trying to tell us. The outgoing team members told us that they were asking for pens. I thought that was strange. Little kids usually want candy or a toy or something, but for those kids the most important thing was a pen so that they could use it for school and become more literate. I gave away so many pens that I rarely had one when I needed it. When thinking of something good to do for the country I thought that getting pens and pencils to the kids would be a good idea. I told my mom about it, and she decided to get involved and conduct a pen drive for the kids. For a month or two, my mom worked with local organizations and managed to get tens of thousands of pens shipped to us. One of our hometown banks even held a pen drive and drop-off box to help. It was a great community project, and to thank them we presented the bank with an American flag flown on Bin Laden's house along with a picture of our team and a thank-you message. The flag, picture and thank-you message are still hanging on the entrance wall to the bank. Later I made a connection with a gentleman in Reno, Nevada, who engaged his local Rotary Club and sent thousands of pens to me, as well. I became known in Jalalabad as Captain Kalam (Captain Pen). It may have been a small gesture, but it felt good to do something for the kids, and they seemed to genuinely appreciate it.

Handing Out Pens at a Local School

Mom Did Not Know

About midway through my one-year tour, I was asked to do an interview for National Public Radio. I thought that would be cool. Sometimes I forgot how little everyone back home knew about the war in Afghanistan, since everyone was focused on Iraq in 2005. The interviewer asked me questions about our mission and what my team was doing over there. I told him about our adventures in the mountains and the IEDs that we were hit by and about our pen drive. The interview seemed to go pretty well until I gave my mom a call later on. I had not told her about the IEDs or what I was doing on my missions. To save her from dying of worry, I told her that I was in a position where I rarely left the base and was perfectly safe at all times. The truth was that I had picked one of the most dangerous jobs possible and was out in the bush nearly every day we were there. She was quite pissed at me for lying to her, but she understood very well why I had done it. It would not be the last time that I lied to my mom about my whereabouts and missions.

Projects

One of the main responsibilities of a Civil Affairs team is to work with communities to do projects that benefit them. During the year, our team did several projects with different communities. The most prevalent project was the Construction Trades Training Center (CTTC), a joint project done with USAID. Together we constructed a school that helped train electricians, plumbers, masons, carpenters, painters, and some other trades. It was a very successful program that trained thousands of people in those trades over several years. I became close friends with the guys who ran the CTTC and even worked with them in future programs years later. That project may have been the single most important project that we could have done for Nangarhar and surrounding provinces. Our team also worked on rehabilitation of irrigation and road systems; built schools, government buildings, and micro-hydroelectric systems; and some other small community projects. I used the knowledge gained from building those projects to help me plan for projects in future years as a civilian aid worker.

Students Learning Plumbing at the CTTC

Other NGOs and IOs

Afghanistan was so thoroughly destroyed after decades of war that all pillars of society were decimated. In response, the international aid effort for Afghanistan was massive. Hundreds of non-governmental organizations (NGOs) blanketed the country. They tried to help with everything from health, education, and refugees to basic infrastructure and governance. The city of Jalalabad in the Nangarhar Province was where all aid workers in the eastern part of Afghanistan lived and worked.

There were so many aid agencies working in Afghanistan — with hundreds in the Nangarhar Province alone — that it was insane. Although everyone was there trying their best to make a difference, the sheer number of organizations made it difficult to coordinate efforts. To me, it was a crazy mess that should have been organized and streamlined. The U.N. representatives in the province did their best to corral the mass of aid agencies into working groups by sector so that everyone could coordinate their efforts and avoid overlap. It was helpful, but since it lacked any real authority, not every organization attended.

When I attended the health sector meeting as the head of Civil Affairs for the province I was quickly yelled at by the health sector aid agencies. They were upset that we would go out in the outlying area villages sometimes and conduct one-day mini clinics. It disrupted the villagers getting care from their regular clinics that those aid agencies sponsored. They had finally gotten people to pay 1 Afghani (about 2 cents) to the clinics, but since our one-day clinic was free it led to villagers demanding free care from the aid agency clinics. I apologized for the issue and explained that we were trying to gain some trust with the villagers. They were not having it and continued to castigate me. Then I told them that we would only do such one-day clinics in areas where there was little-to-no representation from the aid agency clinics, mostly in dangerous, remote areas. They agreed with that. I tried to smooth things over by saying, "Okay, you got your licks in on me, now tell me how I can help your efforts instead of hamper them." That made the room fall silent, as they really just came there to complain rather than coordinate. Finally, one aid worker spoke up: "Could you provide generators to the clinics? They desperately need power to keep the refrigerators going, so medicines stay cool." I agreed I would look into trying to get generators to help their efforts. The mood quickly became more cordial, and we actually got some things accomplished.

The Taj

On Thursday evenings, all of the NGO workers got together for drinks at a big house outside of Jalalabad. We called that house the Taj, since it was rather lavish and huge, with a nice pool and tiki bar built by the U.N. road-building team back in 2005. The guys who lived at the Taj were all former military guys from New Zealand and Australia, with a few others sprinkled in. We had a great relationship with them and were often invited to the Thursday night parties. Some of the NGO workers did not take kindly to military guys attending the parties, since it could make them a target for bad guys and soil their reputation for independence. Although it was a valid point, trust me, the second bombs and guns went off in their area they would quickly love for us to be around.

We went to the parties in a pretty funny way. First, in order to get out of the base I would put in a mission plan I called "Operation Light Bright." The objective was to assess the streetlights in the city to see if they were working. We did accomplish that mission only on the road to the party. Sure, it was a little childish, but damn it was fun. When we reached the gates of the Taj we could not come into the U.N. compound with weapons, so we improvised. We would take the large guns off of the turrets of our Humvees and throw them in the trunks. We would then hide all of our other weapons, take off our uniform tops, and walk around with t-shirts and our baseball caps on. We got along pretty well with everyone else because we were very laid-back and just wanted to feel normal for a few hours. Since Soldiers were not allowed to drink alcohol we had to ensure that we kept it cool. However, some of the civilians we brought with us were not so cool. On more than one occasion we brought home some of the civilians completely passed out drunk. It was a great secret mission we did every few weeks that helped the year go by a little faster, and we made some good friends in the process.

Joint Mission

One of the missions that we completed in the fall of 2005 was a joint mission between my Civil Affairs team and the U.S. Special Forces team that operated in the province. The mission was a five-day operation to go into the most dangerous areas of the province, and work with the local population to talk about their issues and hopefully develop good relations with them. The first district we went to was the Khogyani District. There we had arranged a meeting with all of the major elders and stakeholders in the district. The Special Forces team commander spoke first, telling the elders about how we wanted to increase security, and work with them to stop terrorism and insurgency in the area. The elders began to speak one at a time, scolding and shouting at us, saying that we were coming into their homes and taking their women and invading their privacy for no reason. They screamed that the district was very safe, and that we were always welcome there, and should come and build development projects in the area for them. The Special Forces team commander looked at me, and I asked, "Are you buying any of this?" He made a funny face and said, "Hell no, we were attacked in this district a couple weeks ago!"

The Special Forces team commander then turned the meeting over to me. I stood up in front of those 50 elders and discussed how we would like to come and work with communities to improve their lives through infrastructure projects and other activities that could help foster peace and goodwill. That seemed to help the situation a little bit, but the elders did continue to show their frustration with the unannounced intrusions into their compounds. The Khogyani District was known for its support of the insurgency and anti-government sentiment. We moved on to our next objective, which was to take over the compound of a well-known anti-government insurgency leader. That insurgency leader was known for carrying out operations that killed U.S. troops and was involved in a power struggle with the leadership in the Nangarhar Province. We arrived at his compound, which essentially was a large square area with 15-foot-high mud walls and a large gate. There was very little else inside of the compound. A small family was renting the place and apparently living in the little tower room in the compound. We asked the family to relocate, and they did.

After we moved into the compound, we began planning a mission to attack some illegal Taliban checkpoints that had started up in the area. We linked up with a local Afghan National Army company that was going to work with us on our operations. The Afghan commander wanted to throw a dinner for us and slaughtered a lamb and prepared a nice feast for the evening. I was never a big fan of lamb, or any Afghan food for that matter, but it would be very rude to refuse to eat with our hosts. All of our team members that evening sat with our Afghan counterparts and had a great time eating, laughing, and getting to know each other. The next day, however, was a different story. As soon as I woke up I realized I had food poisoning. I could barely move and had to have the medic come over to give me two IVs and some Cipro and help me get to a secluded area to use as a makeshift bathroom in the middle of the desert. When I got back to our meeting area everybody began to laugh and make fun of me, calling me "weak genes." However, by midday I was feeling fine and was finally able to take water and food. About the time that I was feeling better, one by one everyone else began to fall ill, and the compound looked more like an infirmary than a military installation. Thanks to everyone's food poisoning, we ended up scrapping the mission for that evening. Over the next few days, we went to four different districts, meeting with local elders and talking with community members. It was a good five days to familiarize ourselves with one of the most dangerous areas of Afghanistan.

MEDCAPs

One of the activities that I had helped plan for the province was conducting medical civilian assistance programs out in rural areas — better known as MEDCAPs. Basically, they consisted of holding a one-day free clinic out in areas that had no access to medical care. A special team of doctors, nurses, and medics with a lot of equipment and medicine came to our base. It was my job to help coordinate getting them to the field and dealing with the local population to ensure that they knew about the clinic, as well as that the government officials would be able to identify a place that we would be able to set up. We did one MEDCAP in the most rural area of the Nangarhar Province called Hesarak District. The governor of that district was Abdul Haq, who became a good friend throughout my years in Afghanistan. As we set up the tents and the medical equipment for the one-day free clinic, hundreds of local citizens came from miles around and lined up to see the doctors, many for the first time in a while. Speaking with the doctors afterward was a shocking experience.

Out there, there were so many illnesses and issues that are found in very few places in the world. Polio, which has been eradicated from nearly the entire world, was still a problem in rural Afghanistan. Due to familial marriages, there was an extraordinary amount of birth defects that went untreated. But one of the most shocking things that I had heard was when one man brought his wife to the doctor to find out why she had not become pregnant. The man said that he was very upset with his wife that she had not become pregnant, and he had apparently been beating her due to his frustration. When the OB-GYN exam was complete it turned out that the reason she could not become pregnant was that she had never had *vaginal* sexual intercourse. I will not go into any further detail on it, as I think you get the idea. Issues like that make you very much appreciate basic sexual education in the West.

Ladies Receiving Medicine for Their Children at the MEDCAP

Meeting Government Officials

The provincial leadership consisted of the governor and his staff, as well as several directors, such as the director of power, director of irrigation, director of reconstruction and rural development, and the like. In 2005, many of those directors were men who had little education and knowledge of their areas. However, some were quite bright and ready to make a difference. There was also limited funding for infrastructure, staff, or materials, so those directors had restricted power to effect change even if they had wanted to. Most funding and assistance came from the many aid agencies stationed throughout the country. When I would meet with those government officials some would simply blow me off unless I had money or projects to support them. Others would seek me out hoping for some guidance or mentorship to help them figure out what to do in their jobs. It was strange being a 30-year-old captain in the U.S. Army trying to show a 60-year-old Afghan man how to do simple tasks, or how to organize and plan a strategy for his department. As the years went by those directors would become more educated, and many were able to do great things for their province.

Corruption

Illicit activity and corruption were so rampant in Afghanistan that it was hard to see when or where it could be stopped. From former President Karzai's family right down to the village elder, it seemed that everyone wanted to try to scam a buck wherever possible. After 30 years of war and instability, it would seem only reasonable that everyone wanted to get anything they could because it would only be a matter of time before the next crisis hit. I remember that my interpreter would go to the store to get some food for me, and I later found out that he was charging me double the price and pocketing the difference. It was cheap to begin with by Western standards, but it was just the principle of it that was strange, since he was paid well and really did not seem to need the extra money. But when people are in a crisis mindset all of the time, I guess it makes sense to get whatever you can when it is available.

Trimming the Tree

Nangarhar was made up of 22 districts, however, there were also tribal divisions aside from the government, and they arguably had much more power over what happened out in the rural areas. One part of Afghan society that was important to remember was that you had to try to keep everyone happy and treat everyone the same as much as possible. If one tribe was getting more than others, it became a real source of tension. Afghans call that balance "trimming the tree." They said you have to make sure that if you do a little on this side you have to do a little on the other side to keep the tree in balance. I always thought that was a good analogy and never forgot it.

One example of that, on a small scale, hit us one day. When we were going on missions to the rural areas we would often give out some gifts to the population. One of those gifts was windup radios that needed no electrical hookup. They had a battery that was charged by winding a small crank several times to get about a half hour of listening time. It was perfect for rural areas where there was no television or newspapers, and radio was one of the few mass communication mediums. When we would attempt to give those out in public areas, we would be inundated with people rushing the trucks to get one before they were gone. It was always a fiasco, so we asked the local elders to distribute them to those who needed them most. Sometimes the elders would say that since we did not have enough for everyone it would be best to give them to no one so that it did not cause fighting. One elder said, "I understand what you are trying to do, but you are making problems for me in my village. You have to trim the tree." All of these little nuggets of wisdom helped shape my future strategies.

Nanawati in Sherzad and Another IED

After the IED attacks on my team and other attacks on the local Marines, the military commanders in the region decided to have a large meeting with the Afghan leaders in the Sherzad District, one of the most dangerous areas. The meeting consisted of driving out to the district with the governor, Gul Agha Sherzai, and his large entourage, and asking the local people to grant us Nanawati — an Afghan custom of asking for their protection when we went out to their areas. It seemed strange for members of the most powerful army in the world to ask local people for protection, but the bottom line was that we had very few troops there at the time, and the local people knew who the bad guys were. We were going to need to work together to bring stability, or it was never going to come. I was skeptical of the move, since that particular area was filled with ties to the Taliban and other insurgent groups, but I kept an open mind and thought it could not hurt to engage them on the issue. The one thing that I was concerned about was that anytime we set up a meeting in advance and told the local population when and where we were going it gave insurgents a perfect opportunity to set up an ambush, usually in the form of IEDs along our route.

The meeting was kind of a debacle. It seemed that the local leaders were more interested in yelling at the governor and military for not doing more development work in the area. By the time the commander started discussing local protection from insurgents, the crowd was already hostile and not listening. Needless to say, our request for Nanawati seemed to fall on deaf ears. While on the road on the way back from the meeting, an IED hidden in a tree went off right above the truck in front of me. Luckily the bomb's fuse was defective, and the actual explosive charge did not go off. If it had, the gunner sticking out of the roof surely would have been killed. It was another close call and thankfully our last.

Parliamentary Elections

As I had mentioned earlier, being the Civil Affairs officer meant that anything having to do with civilians was my responsibility. So, when the parliamentary elections took place across Afghanistan in 2005 and a military liaison was needed to work with the U.N. for a couple of weeks I got tapped for that role, too. However, it was a role I was happy to take on, since it meant wearing civilian clothes, driving in regular cars, talking to other expats, and doing something special. Another Civil Affairs officer and I were sent down the road to live in a U.N. compound with a large group of U.N. election supervisors and election security personnel from all over the world.

It was a great experience working with people from Britain, Australia, New Zealand, Thailand, and other countries. The U.N. security officer was my boss for that role. He was a former Australian commando with a great sense of humor. Together we planned how to get election ballots safely to all corners of eastern Afghanistan, secure the vote, and then retrieve the ballots. That would not be easy to do in a place where roads were insecure, in terrible condition, and sometimes nonexistent. Everything was used, from large truck convoys to donkeys to try to get ballots to all polling sites. One area in particular was very challenging. Getting ballots to the Nuristan Province, where there were no real roads, no real government presence, and was very insecure. We often joked that getting ballots up there made the infamous "charge of the light brigade" look like a brilliant military strategy by comparison. Nonetheless, overall the election went off with few security issues, and we breathed a sigh of relief when it was over.

Election fraud was rampant in several areas. Some polling places actually had incidents where a policeman would break the seal on the ballot box and stuff the box full of ballots all marked with one candidate's name. Those ballots were easily identified, since the ballots were so large that they had to be folded multiple times to fit into the slot at the top of the box. Broken seals and unfolded ballots were easily identified and quarantined. There were multiple complaints of fraud by all sides, mostly because so many candidates were trying to rig the election and then blame the fraud on their competitors. That created huge problems for the U.N. election monitors who did their best to ensure fairness. In the end, parliament members were all chosen and seated as the first elected parliament in Afghanistan in recent memory. There was an era of optimism around the election, and many Afghans had a sense that there was a chance for peace and democracy in their country for the first time in their lifetimes.

Roads Working Group

The guys on our team were true professionals who cared about the mission that we were doing and honestly wanted to be part of the solution there. One of the team members, King, was a very smart guy and realized that an area that really needed a coordinated effort on was road building. He took it upon himself to develop a working group to take all government and non-government agencies that deal with road building and get them organized and working efficiently. That working group became a huge success and carried on for years. The coordination allowed for the rebuilding and paving of hundreds of miles of roads in the Nangarhar Province. Sometimes the most important thing that infrastructure builders need is organization and a swift kick in the ass to get moving. King's working group did that for roads.

Our Exit and Handover

One of the biggest problems that all military units have is that when they leave the country all knowledge and information leaves with them. It is important to ensure that the new team that takes over is set up for success by providing them good information and a good handover program. We experienced a terrible handover, with very little information left for us and nothing in a form that would help us going forward. We were determined to be different when we changed over with the new team. As a Civil Affairs team we knew how important it was to know where things were, who the important people were, how to do projects, and how to interact with the public. At that time, Google Earth had just come out, and one of the guys realized that it was a great way to document where all of the major infrastructure was in the province. We mapped out all of the schools, clinics, roads, mosques, government buildings, and other important places. We created handover documents and briefings to help ensure that the new team had the knowledge it would need to carry on after we left.

As we left Nangarhar on a helicopter to take us to Bagram Airfield to meet up with the rest of our unit and prepare to go home, I had a satisfied feeling that we had done the best we could over the year, and I was excited to get back to Florida and school. The helicopter flight took us over the mountains, and for a bit I had an eerie feeling that we were going to be shot down or that something terrible was going to happen to us at the last minute. Thankfully, we landed at Bagram without problem, and we could finally take a breath and relax.

We met up with all of the teams coming back from around the country, and it was great sharing stories of our time there. Feeling that our mission was successful, I was surprised to hear from members of nearly every other team that they were very unhappy with their missions over the year, and felt that their time there was awful and that their teams were in chaos much of the time. That was disappointing, since it seemed that much of the problem stemmed from poor leadership and low morale. I was just happy to be headed home with no casualties and knowing my team did its very best. I never put on a military uniform again. And I was sure that I would not be setting foot in Afghanistan ever again, but I was quite wrong.

CHAPTER 2. COUNTERNARCOTICS

After getting home to Florida and starting school again, I realized that there was literally nobody that I could talk to about my experience in Afghanistan. Being the only combat veteran in my class, no one could understand or even vaguely comprehend what I saw and did. I felt a little lonely and did not talk about Afghanistan very much aside from a few close friends. It seemed as though I did not really fit in where I was, and as much as I tried to pour myself into school and work I was just bored and longing for a new challenge. That challenge would be coming in the form of a phone call only a few months after getting home.

In January of 2007, I received a call from a friend I had met in Afghanistan. I was in class when the phone rang, and since I saw that it was from overseas I walked out of class and answered it. "Chris, it's Bob. Hey, can you be in Afghanistan in two weeks?" I thought he was nuts. I also thought why in the hell would I want to go back there but that I would indulge him since he was calling from Europe. I said, "What the heck are you talking about? No way in hell am I going back there!" He explained that he had been offered a job running a counternarcotics team, but he could not take the job and was offering it to me. He told me about the substantial paycheck, and the job seemed like a cool challenge. I walked down to the registrar's office and immediately withdrew from school. Two weeks later I was on a plane back to Afghanistan, but that time as a civilian contractor for the U.S. State Department counternarcotics program.

Growing opium poppies and processing heroin was and is one of the largest industries in Afghanistan. Over 90 percent of the world's illicit opiates comes from Afghanistan, breeding corruption and funding terrorism. I learned that well during my military experience there. I was proud to be going back to hopefully make a difference and to try to stop some of the production of the deadly drug. I knew that doing so would be difficult, if not impossible, but I figured it was a good challenge, and the pay was great. I had no idea what was going to happen or where I would be in Afghanistan, but I figured what the heck, I had nothing to lose at the time.

The big security contractor company that I was working for was the type that often wins large government contracts. It was so large that its employees were really only known by their employee number, not by name. I arrived in Afghanistan in February of 2007, having no idea that I would be spending most of the next decade living there. The company's security team picked me up and quickly drove through the streets of Kabul to the company's large compound that looked like a fortress. At lunch, I met with the company program manager and the State Department representative in charge of overseeing the program. After sharing some war stories and having a few laughs, I finally said, "So what is it you guys want me to do for you?" They both kind of chuckled and said, "Just go do what you do." I was kind of surprised that they had few expectations, no guidance for me, and did not seem to take the program too seriously. At least I felt at ease that I really could not fail if there were no expectations.

I was assigned to the Helmand Province, the single worst place in Afghanistan at the time. The province was overrun with Taliban, and the government there was completely inept and corrupt. The Helmand Province in Afghanistan in 2007 grew nearly 40 percent of the world's illicit opium/heroin. That insane amount of drug growth fueled corruption and terrorism and was a major thorn in the side of all efforts to stem the dangerous heroin epidemic throughout the world. My job was to advise the team of Afghans that was in charge of working with the local government to stop farmers from growing opium poppies by conducting information campaigns, working with aid agencies to assist in providing alternative crops, and monitoring the government's efforts to eradicate opium poppy fields. We were supposed to do all of that with almost no funding for activities and little authority to direct anyone to do anything. It was a fool's errand in a place that had no intention of stopping opium poppy cultivation and almost zero incentive to change anything.

The day after my arrival in Afghanistan I had finished breakfast and was getting ready to fly from Kabul in the north to my new home in Helmand. The security lead asked me if I was ready. I was feeling a little lightheaded and feverish, but I thought it was just jetlag, so I said, "Yep, just let me grab my gear." I then suddenly turned my head and threw up off of the side of the dining hall stairs. Another case of food poisoning had gotten me. I turned back to him and said, "Well maybe after a trip to the clinic for some Cipro." After a little rest, I caught my flight to Helmand and was picked up from a secluded airstrip outside of the provincial capital of Lashkargah. That city was actually considered a "Little America" because back in the 1960s the U.S. government helped build the town while constructing a huge dam nearby that supplies much of the irrigation water and electricity to southern Afghanistan. Many of the old houses in the city looked like the 1960s brick ranch-style houses straight out of an American suburb.

The place was incredibly dangerous, and just a month before my arrival the security team was hit by a suicide bomber who jumped on the roof of one of the armored trucks and detonated his explosive vest. The vest contained a massive amount of explosives and dozens of ball bearings. The explosion destroyed the front of the target truck and several of the ball bearings breached the armor of the other vehicle in front of the target vehicle, injuring the driver. Luckily no one was killed. The team was on high alert and expected to be attacked again. The security team was made up of Nepalese Gurkhas — soldiers who are well known for their bravery and discipline. Those guys were no different. They were tough, yet always smiling and courteous. The banner over their dorm room said, "It is better to die than be a coward!" I felt quite sure those guys would always stand and fight if need be. We lived in a small compound in the middle of the city with 10-foot walls, secured gates, and at least 10 well-armed Gurkhas at any one time. I felt that we were well prepared for any attack.

We arrived at the compound, and I met the British gentleman, Ray, whom I was replacing. I also met the Afghan team that I was going to be advising. The Afghan team was comprised of a team leader, Mr. Mani; one information officer named Ahmed; two alternative development officers named Mohammad and Hashim; and two eradication monitors named Yasir and Mahmood. The group was a nice compilation of men who were trying their best despite a tough role in the worst place. Ray was an older British veteran and a genuinely nice fellow. We got along well, and he showed me the day-to-day workings of my job.

He also took me over to the nearby British base about three miles away. The British military was in charge of Helmand, and their base in Lashkargah was our safe haven in case of attack. I was given a room at the base, as well, that Ray had occupied for the past year. It was good to be able to attend meetings at the base with the military to share intelligence and information and keep up to date on the security situation in the province. Since the military was well consigned to the base, it liked getting on-the-ground information from my team and I that we received from our daily interactions with the general population.

During those daily meetings at the base, I learned that the British military had a hugely different outlook on the war than a former U.S. Army officer like myself. One thing that shocked me was that the British seemed content with allowing the Taliban to take over territory and hold it. Their strategy seemed to be that they would let the Taliban run wild in the rural areas, while they would attempt to hold the key cities and major roads. That was something the U.S. military would never accept. Knowingly allowing the enemy to have a safe haven and not doing anything about it was nuts in my opinion. I guess the British did not want to bring in the troops required to take on that threat. It would not be long before the U.S. Marines would step into Helmand to bail out the British and retake the areas that had been ceded to the Taliban.

A few weeks into my assignment in Helmand, the commander of the base pulled me aside at a meeting and said that they would be taking away my room there because they needed the space for others. It kind of pissed me off, since I was helping to coordinate a lot of information, and driving back and forth to their nightly meetings was not a very safe thing to do at the time. I stopped going to the meetings, and, unfortunately, the information flow stopped along with that. Isolated on our compound, the nights were pretty quiet and eerie. It was easy to feel lonely and far away from the world, but I tried to focus on work and see where I could make a difference.

I sat the team down and tried to get a sense of where we were and what our strategy would be going forward. The governor, local leaders, and the general population had no appetite to stop illegal poppy cultivation, and it seemed that nothing would change that. Power brokers all over the country owned the poppy fields in Helmand. Many elected officials, including governors, parliament members, and warlords, made millions from the poppy fields there. It was like a mafia, where no law enforcement officer would dare touch the poppy fields if he wanted to live. My first meeting was with the team leader, who basically said that the current governor of the province was corrupt and did not care about the poppy growth in Helmand. It was so bad that even the side yards of some of the houses in the city were filled with poppies. I thought that if people can grow them in the middle of town right in plain sight of the police station, then there was a real problem. I then sat down with the information officer, the alternative development officers, and the eradication monitors to see what the situation was with each of their respective areas.

The information officer, Ahmed, was a younger guy who was ambitious and wanted to be a journalist. He would often post op-eds in the local paper calling out corruption and wrongdoing by the government. He had multiple threats lobbied against him from those who wanted him silenced. I have to give him credit for his bravery. He had almost no budget to run anti-poppy information campaigns and had to rely on an annual poster campaign, where the state department would send us anti-poppy posters trying to dissuade farmers from growing poppies. The silly thing was that the posters were all written in the Dari language, whereas Helmand was a Pashto-speaking region. The posters might as well have been in Greek. Since most people were illiterate anyway, I suppose it did not really matter.

Ahmed also tried to get out anti-poppy messages through the one place where people would listen: the mosques. He tried to convince the local mullahs (pastors) to preach about the dangers and spiritual corrosion of growing opium poppies that kill and destroy lives all over the world. I was surprised when he told me that the mullahs were some of the most corrupt people and actually wanted to be paid handsomely to preach that message. He said that the mullahs were essentially for sale, and the poppy business owned them. The feeling was that the drugs were mostly going to Westerners anyway, so who cares if their lives were affected. The truth was that there were over a million opium addicts in Afghanistan, which only had a population of 35 million. They were killing their own people, too.

The next group to focus on was the alternative development officers. They, like the information officer, had no funds to do anything. They spent their days talking to mostly aid agencies, which were trying to conduct projects to help the farmers transition to other crops and stop growing opium poppies. With Helmand being such a dangerous place, there were few projects taking place, and the ones that were operating there were not having much success. Like most programs in Afghanistan, there was a huge lack of strategy. Aid agencies would come in and try to introduce some new farming methods, different crops, and ways to irrigate crops better, but there did not seem to be an overall plan. The huge irrigation systems in Helmand were also in a horrible state of disrepair, leading to uncertain water conditions for crops.

The largest aid program focused on working with farmers to grow vegetables and cotton, which used to be a staple crop in that area. I went to that program's office to discuss its strategy and was not surprised to see that it was not making much headway. The program had enlisted some very old gentlemen from the U.S. and other Western countries. They did not seem very motivated by the work they were doing, and during the meeting two of the old men fell asleep while we were talking. It was quite discouraging. The biggest problem was that opium from poppies yielded a much higher price than any other crop and grew very well in the dry conditions of Helmand, so getting farmers to switch to something else was a hard sell.

One particular program tried to get farmers to switch to growing chili peppers. It conducted demonstration farms to teach farmers how to grow them and tried to set up an export market. That crop would have a high yield and would offer a good income to a farmer who grew it. Several farmers came into our office to speak with the chili program's manager. I watched as several farmers sat down with the manager to compare crops, and he wrote out the math on a piece of paper. The farmers concluded that even though the chili peppers were a good option, it was still more profitable to grow poppies. They simply did not care that they were growing an illegal drug, and with no repercussions from law enforcement or the government there was no incentive to change. With that type of attitude toward alternative crops, it seemed there was little that the aid agencies could do except help the few farmers who had a conscience and wanted to grow other crops.

The last part of our team was the eradication monitors. Those two guys again had no budget or authority, and their job was to check on and report on the government's efforts to eradicate the poppy fields by cutting them down. The idea was to scare farmers into stopping opium poppy cultivation by threatening to cut their fields down, leaving them without an income. Although the approach sounded aggressive and tough, it really was not.

The U.S. State Department tried to intervene by contracting a U.S. company to work with the Afghan government to lead eradication efforts in Helmand. The team was called the Poppy Eradication Force. That team of both American and Afghan brave security officers would assemble a large contingent of tractors and men to go out to poppy fields and forcibly cut them down. The team had the resources and ability to put a huge dent in the number of poppy fields if they were allowed to do their work efficiently. However, they had the mandate to take orders from the government, which would decide what fields the team would cut down. Since many government officials owned those poppy fields and did not want them cut down, the team was often sent on missions where it would drive all day past hundreds of acres of poppy fields to arrive at a small area that it was allowed to cut down. The targeted fields were often those of poor farmers, who did not or could not pay the bribes needed to protect their fields. Or the farmers would choose whose field would be sacrificed, and that farmer would get reimbursed by others.

It was an extremely dangerous job, and the team was often attacked, and its equipment destroyed. The team was only able to complete a small amount of the eradication compared to what was possible. The head of that team was a burly gentleman, who was tough as nails and a good leader. He was frustrated but did the best he could with what he had. I had to give him credit for his courage to take on such a dangerous and fleeting task. One member of the team told me that as they drove past poppy fields some of the Afghan team members would tell him which government official owned which poppy field. Of course, the team was forbidden from cutting those fields down, adding to the frustration and feeling that the eradication effort was a farce and would not really change anything in Helmand. To this day, Helmand remains one of the world's biggest producers of illegal opium and heroin, feeding the worldwide epidemic.

I spent about six months in Helmand, dreading it and wishing that I was back in Nangarhar, where I had been stationed with the military. I felt that I would be able to actually produce some results if I was there. The situation in Helmand seemed impossible, and I was wasting my time being there. I was so frustrated that I looked for other jobs and was actually offered a few, but none of them seemed to be what I really wanted, which was a chance to make a difference. My prayers were soon answered. The program was about to change companies. A new company won the contract, and soon we were given a choice to either leave, or stay and work for the new company. I was happy to stay on with the new company, but I asked that I be moved to Nangarhar as a stipulation of my new contract. The company agreed, and I was soon on my way back to the city of Jalalabad in Nangarhar, where I felt that I could do some good.

The new company was a much smaller firm, and instead of being just a number everyone knew your name and seemed to genuinely care about your well-being. The leadership was a lot more approachable and just outright cooler to hang out with. Instead of having a huge compound outside of Kabul with massive security, the headquarters was a large house in the middle of Kabul, where you felt welcome and part of the team. The job was essentially the same except for a few things. First, we got a lot of vacation time, working eight weeks and then getting two weeks off to go anywhere in the world we wanted. I used my vacation time well, traveling to Thailand, Dubai, India, and all over Europe, eventually even meeting my future wife while in Bulgaria. Second, the security team was made up of local Afghans instead of Nepalese Gurkhas. To many of the expats, that was scary, as they feared that some of the local Afghans might be influenced by the Taliban, who wished them harm. I was a little hesitant at first, but soon the Afghans proved themselves to be loyal and trustworthy.

I was happy as hell being back in a familiar place with a good job, and I was ready to make a difference. When I arrived back in Nangarhar, I immediately met the new team, and I could tell that it was going to be a better experience. Nangarhar was much safer than Helmand, and, although certainly there were rampant corruption and security concerns, there were some government officials who were serious about stopping poppy cultivation and bringing economic growth to the province. I already knew several of the main power brokers in the province, and since I had just left the military post there a year ago I figured I could make some friends at the base and lend them a hand with my experience.

The New Team

The Nangarhar counternarcotics team that I was advising consisted of Mr. Nani, the team leader; Qani, my interpreter; Ahmed, the administrator; Yosef and Yani, the eradication monitors; Lak and Hadi, the alternative development officers; and Mohammed, the information officer. It was a much more skilled group than the Helmand team, and since the area was safer we were able to go out in the field together more, which helped us get a better sense of what was happening with poppy cultivation and how the farmers were feeling about changes happening there.

I first met with the information officer, an unapproachable guy who seemed to dislike foreigners and was not happy to talk much about his work. Over the course of the year, he would conduct the standard poster campaign but also radio interviews to spread anti-poppy messages, polls out in the districts to try and understand how the farmers were thinking and what they were planning to grow, and work with the mullahs to try to spread anti-poppy messages during the Friday prayers at the mosques. Throughout the year, the U.S. State Department provided hundreds of prayer rugs and loudspeaker systems for the mosques as a gesture of good will. The information officer and team leader led the effort to distribute them to great fanfare. Altogether we had a pretty good plan for getting out anti-poppy messages, and the information officer did a decent job.

The eradication monitors had a much better job in Nangarhar, since they had freedom of movement all over the province. They helped the information officer with polls and distributing messages around the province, and when the poppy season arrived they tried to identify where poppies were being grown in the province and monitored the government's eradication efforts. Unlike Helmand, Nangarhar did not have a large U.S.-run eradication force; instead, the provincial counternarcotics team worked with the police to identify and cut down poppy fields themselves. The prior year, Nangarhar was second only to Helmand in the amount of poppy grown, so stopping it would still be a daunting task.

The alternative development officers, Lak and Hadi, ended up being my two closest associates on the team. Their job was to understand the aid agencies working out in the field and report on the kinds of activities that were happening, and to see where more could be done to help farmers move from growing poppies to growing other crops. Throughout my next two years of advising the team, I would learn a lot from the field missions that Lak, Hadi, and I would go on, which shaped my understanding of the country more than anything else.

Working with the Military PRT

After meeting the team and getting situated, I next wanted to go to the PRT military base, where I had served a little more than a year before. When I arrived there, I was welcomed and met the Civil Affairs team that had just taken over for the team that I had transitioned with the year prior. It was a shame that I had not arrived just weeks before and could have met up with the guys I had turned our duties over to. The new team members were getting situated into their roles in a country they did not know, and they were happy to sit down with me and let me brief them on what I knew about the province. I had written a handbook published by DBS International that each of them had received prior to deploying, so some of the leaders knew my name from reading it.

I was very interested in getting my hands on all of the information that my team had collected and turned over to the team that succeeded us. Shockingly, all of that information was lost, and the new team had no idea where it was or that it even existed. What made me even madder was that the new team was trying to recreate all of that same data that we had collected. I felt like the hundreds of hours that we had spent creating those important documents were a complete waste of time. It also meant that every year a military team would come in and try to do their jobs, only to transition out and have another team do the same thing. What a waste of time! It was no wonder that every team got very little done there. Instead of a 20-year war, it was more like 20 one-year wars, with little to show for it but wasted blood and money.

Throughout the next couple of years, I tried hard to help the military units stationed there, since they were trying their best to bring stability and security to the province. I was asked by the PRT commander to sit in on some of their meetings, since I could brief them on the poppy situation in the province and let them in on any issues that I found out in the districts. Since the PRT was also building some projects, such as schools and roads, out in the districts, it was good information for me to know, as well. There was one meeting where the PRT commander walked in, sat down, and said, "What am I buying today?" The Civil Affairs officer said, "Well, we were driving around a village in one of the districts, and kids were sitting on the ground in a makeshift school, so we would like to build a school there!" I was not sure I should speak up, since I knew a lot of military officers were thin-skinned (having been one of them). But I wanted to help, so I chimed in, "Have you met the director of education for the province?" The officer said, "Well, no." I said, "Just an idea for you since I know you guys are new here, but the education director for the province is a really smart guy, and he now has a complete list of all of the schools by priority that he needs built. Some schools out there are not actual, registered schools, so you may want to talk to him before building anything. Just an idea, I've been in your shoes before." The officer looked down like I had just insulted him, although, I was as cordial and polite as I could be. The commander moved on quickly to the next order of business, and I was never invited back to a meeting there again.

The PRT ended up building several projects that were very useful, such as rural roads that definitely helped the province in many ways, from security to trade. Some of the other projects were complete failures because there was not a coordinated effort between the government and the local leaders like there should have been. It reminded me of some of the mistakes I made while working at the PRT. Nobody wanted to take advice or learn from the mistakes of past units, so we just continued to move one step forward and two steps back. With the amount of money the U.S. government spent there, we could have built every road, school, clinic, irrigation system, and power grid needed twice over.

On my way back from the meeting at the PRT, I was driving to my compound next to the governor's house in the middle of town. When I arrived, there was a group of large U.S. military vehicles stuck, trying to get into the gate leading to the governor's house. I needed to enter the same gate to get to my compound. My driver and I stopped about 30 yards behind the military trucks so that those guys would not be spooked by us, or think we were a threat and mistakenly fire on us. We were driving an armored SUV and should have been recognized as part of the government, but I was not going to tempt fate with a military unit that was new to Afghanistan. After waiting for about 5 minutes while the Soldiers desperately tried to get their huge new armored vehicles through the small gate, I thought I would try to lend a hand so I could get home.

I walked slowly out of my truck and toward the convoy, with no weapons and my hands open to my sides so that the Soldiers could clearly see that I was not a threat. I thought a blonde-haired white guy wearing Western clothes and calling to them in English, "Hey, guys can I help you?" would be another hint that I was not an enemy, but, nonetheless, they pointed rifles at me and told me to stop. I froze and told them I live there and just wanted to get through the gate, and maybe I could help them find whom they were looking for. They let me walk up to the gate, where a very upset major was waiving her hands and shouting in frustration, "I am here to see Masood, the governor's chief of staff, but I don't know where he is. He is supposed to be here!" I was surprised to see a high-ranking military officer acting so hysterically in front of her own troops, who just kind of shook their heads in embarrassment. I offered to call Masood for her, since I knew him well and had his phone number handy. It did not take long, and I got her into the gate.

Field Missions

In order to understand what was happening in the rural districts where poppy was grown, I knew I had to get out on the ground and see things for myself. Although I knew the layout of the province pretty well from spending a year in the Army in Nangarhar, there was only so much I could absorb then from behind an armored truck and wearing 25 pounds of body armor. I needed to get out and walk the terrain and meet people as a normal person. I began by growing a beard to fit in with every other male in the area and wearing Afghan local clothes to blend in better. I began going out on constant field missions with Lak and Hadi to talk to people around the districts. That was no small issue, since there were plenty of bad guys out there who wished me harm.

The three of us would jump in a beat-up Toyota Corolla and go to villages in areas where poppy growth was rampant. We would walk up and down the riverbeds looking at irrigation systems and talking with local farmers. Often we would be walking down a streambed when a local villager would see us and come ask what we were doing. We would say we wanted to see the irrigation system, so the villager would go and get the local murab (guy in charge of the irrigation system). That old man would then send a boy to grab tea and cups, and we would sit in the middle of the streambed drinking green tea and talking about how the system worked. I was intrigued by the centuries-old intricate systems of canals and gates that irrigated all of the fields, fed only by gravity.

Learning About Irrigation Systems with Local Villagers

I soon learned that nearly all of the systems were in a horrible state of disrepair, putting a huge strain on the farmers' ability to grow adequate crop yields. Although several aid agencies were working to rehabilitate the systems, there were over 1,500 individual irrigation systems in Nangarhar alone. At the time of my field missions, less than 10 percent had been even marginally addressed. The need was huge, and we were not meeting it. It was a huge problem for the rural farmers, and they used the issue as an excuse to grow opium poppies. They figured that if we were not going to address their needs then they were going to do whatever they needed to in order to make an acceptable living. It was hard to fault that logic. Decent vegetable crop yields depended upon a reliable amount of water. Unfortunately, opium poppies grow with very little water and are very resilient. I could see that was an issue we were going to need to address more fully if we were going to stop poppy growth.

HERPIS — It's Spreading

After months of missions into the rural districts, walking down streambeds, and sitting for hundreds of cups of tea with local villagers and community leaders, I was starting to really understand the needs in the rural areas where instability, poverty, and poppy growth was happening. Most of our government's efforts in reconstruction were focused on completing a small project in an almost random way. We would build a school here, an irrigation system there, and a greenhouse over there. We did that thinking that those small trinket projects would satisfy the villagers' need to see progress, and they would be happy. But there was no coherent development strategy, and the need was enormous versus the small amount accomplished. Building one school in a district that needs 25 schools does not come close to satisfying the needs. Rebuilding two irrigation systems in a district that needs 50 rebuilt does the same. Worse yet, often those projects could cause instability because villages that did not receive projects were jealous of the villages that did get projects, causing rifts in the community.

I began to form a thesis in my head that if we were to truly get a handle on the development issues in the rural areas we would need to focus on comprehensive development planning. Instead of building a few token projects here and there, we should create complete district development plans that addressed the main issues in the most important sectors. I tried to sell my thesis to anyone who would listen. When I brought my idea to the agriculture team at the PRT I was explaining the idea to a young officer. As I sketched out the idea on a white board, I told him that we should focus on health, education, roads, power, irrigation, and security. For simplicity I simply wrote the first letter of each sector: H-E-R-P-I-S. As I wrote, two guys listening started to chuckle, but I was focused on my speech and did not get the joke. I stopped and said, "What's so funny?" One of the young officers laughed and said, "So this is the herpes plan?" referring to the disease. I looked at the board and started laughing, too, and said, "Well, let's hope it spreads!"

I was sure I was on to a good idea, so I brought the HERPIS plan to the major in charge of operations for the entire eastern region of Afghanistan. I explained how important it was to create real district development plans that all agencies could work from. It was just a matter of sitting down with the district councils and letting them build their plans around the model. That would provide a virtual list of projects that any aid agency or military unit could use as a menu of options to build based on available funds or need. The major loved the idea, and his team actually put together a briefing for the commander of the eastern region based on that idea. The major invited me to the briefing, and I watched as my idea was presented as an example to the commander. When the briefing ended, the commander actually yelled, "Now you guys finally get what I want!" I guess the idea resonated with him. The major stood at the head of the briefing table and turned to me with a grin, happy to take credit for the idea. It did not bother me, as I was just happy to have someone listening.

Nangarhar Inc.

Later in the year, that military unit became invigorated by the concept of comprehensive development planning and even got so ambitious that it built a huge plan at the regional level that they called Nangarhar Inc. The details are too big to go into, but the plan basically tried to address big items needed to make the region into a more modern booming economy. It addressed everything from major highways, railways, sewer systems, airports, bridges, and industrial parks to many other large-ticket items. It was a great blueprint for the next 40 years, but unfortunately would cost over a billion dollars, and no one was willing to pay the bill. I was more interested in actionable plans that could bring immediate relief to the province and address the problems that fostered instability and poppy growing at the lower levels of society, especially the rural areas.

Working with Governor Sherzai

Over the course of all of my time in Afghanistan, Gul Agha Sherzai was the governor of the Nangarhar Province. During my years there, I sat in many meetings with him and was often invited to evening meetings, where it was just a few of us discussing our strategies to stop poppy cultivation and complete development projects for rural areas. He was a stout man, with a short beard and no front teeth. It was rumored that he lost his front teeth biting an enemy in a fight during the civil war. That might just be a myth. He was well known as a former warlord in Kandahar Province before the Taliban takeover in the 1990s, and he became the Kandahar provincial governor after the U.S. military ousted the Taliban in 2001. He had a reputation for brutality and ambition, yet effectiveness.

When Sherzai became governor of Nangarhar in 2004 it was hoped that him being an outsider to the province would help bring about a new start. Governor Sherzai was pretty unpredictable. He could be a calm, thoughtful man, who seemed to want the best for his constituents, but at other times he would rant and rave and walk out of meetings if he did not hear what he wanted. There were understandably mixed reviews from the international community, but in general I got along and appreciated the governor for a few reasons. First, he was serious about stopping poppy cultivation, and was willing to plan and execute a strategy to do it. Second, he was willing to work with the military and international aid community to bring stability to the region without a lot of red tape. He wanted to get stuff done and did not have a lot of tolerance for incompetence. Basically, our goals aligned well. Over my six years in Nangarhar, we developed a good relationship.

Zero Poppies in Nangarhar

In 2007, there was so much opium poppy growing in the Nangarhar Province that it was ranked No. 2 in growth, only behind Helmand. In 2008, Governor Sherzai was determined to shut it down. The polls that we took out in the field showed that there were two main things that might help shut it down. The first was law enforcement. Many farmers were waiting to see if the government would actually enforce the poppy ban and throw farmers in jail for growing it. The second was that the farmers wanted the development projects that had been promised to them if they stopped growing poppy. The government put out the word that they were serious about enforcing the ban. When poppy planting started there were a few farmers who tested the government by planting poppy in their fields. Around 100 farmers were arrested and thrown in jail. That signaled to the other farmers that the government was serious, and very few farmers risked growing poppy. The governor then assembled an eradication force of police officers to find and cut down any remaining poppy fields. The end result was that Nangarhar went from being the second largest grower of poppy to being poppy free in 2008. The government and international community then had to fulfill their role by building development projects to help the farmers as was promised.

Good Performers Initiative

With the 2008 poppy season a success, it was time to reward the farmers of Nangarhar for such a dramatic turnaround. The farmers demanded that they see serious development to help make up for lost revenue they would have gotten from growing poppy. The U.S. State Department awarded $10 million to Nangarhar for building development projects. The problem was that the provincial government was in charge of deciding what projects it wanted and had to manage the funds. It seemed that Governor Sherzai felt that the money should go right into his general fund and that he could do whatever he wanted to with it. That, of course, was unacceptable since many thought he could just pocket the money. There were several meetings to discuss the issue, but no one really took charge.

I stepped in and offered that my team could oversee the projects and funds directly from the State Department. I had plenty of experience running projects from my stint in the military, and the State Department could be more comfortable knowing someone on their team was watching the money to make sure it went to the right place. The governor agreed, and I spent the next month coming up with a plan to use the $10 million to help farmers. I sought the advice of several people in the government, local leaders, and international aid community.

The farmers really wanted to see some serious development, such as dams and reservoirs that could help manage water more efficiently, ensuring they could confidently grow crops with good yields. We certainly had enough money to do it, so I spoke with a U.S. construction company to create a plan for building dams. There were about 10 small dams needed that would have satisfied nearly all of the water demand for the province in the areas that needed it. Unfortunately, each dam would cost about $2 million. There were also over 1,000 small irrigation systems throughout the province that needed to be rebuilt. I thought that would be another good option to focus on. Other options included school building, electricity grid, and rural road construction.

That U.S. State Department was not comfortable giving me $10 million to spend, so they told me I could have control of $2 million, and the rest would be contracted by them in Kabul as soon as the Nangarhar government decided what they wanted to do with it. That sounded like a good deal to me, since I knew we could do a lot of good with $2 million. At the next provincial council meeting, I stood up in front of a packed auditorium and presented my plan to the entire leadership of Nangarhar. It consisted of building four dam and reservoir systems costing around $8 million, and about 100 small irrigation systems spread throughout the districts that would be overseen by my team for $2 million. The leadership liked the idea of building the dams but rejected my proposal to build the irrigation systems since they wanted something sexier. That surprised me, because irrigation was the most important thing to the farmers and was the most requested project. I was hoping that we could quickly build out the 100 irrigation systems and then use that success to lobby for more money.

Micro-hydros

I went back to the drawing board with my team, and we decided that rural electrification would be a good second option, since there was almost no access to power in the rural areas aside from personal diesel generators that cost too much for most farmers. Nangarhar's topography gave it a lot of potential for building small hydroelectric systems. Those "micro-hydros" consisted of building a small reservoir with a tube that ran downhill to a turbine that spun a generator, creating anywhere from 3-60 kilowatts. They could power a small village with lights and allow them to operate small electronics. They were not that hard to build with Afghan engineering, and I had built one before in Nangarhar with my friend Yasir in Darai Nur. We presented a new plan to the leadership that we would work with the rural villages to build as many of those micro-hydros as possible with the $2 million. They loved the idea, so we had to figure out how to quickly build micro-hydros in a serious way.

There were a couple of things that my team lacked to be able to do that. First, we had no engineers to design and manage those projects. We started by hiring two engineers who had the education and experience to build the systems. We did not want to contract out the work, since it would have been more expensive, and the contract process was so ripe for corruption. I wanted to control the process and the money so that no one could ever accuse us of the corruption that I had seen rampant in so many programs. I wanted to be able to open our books to anyone who wanted to look and show them where every dollar was spent.

We decided that the way we would manage the projects was that we would identify the sites and get agreements with the village leadership and director of rural reconstruction and development. We would then purchase all of the materials from local vendors. Next, we would work with the village leadership to ensure that they chose the most needy people to be laborers on the projects. We would keep time sheets, which our engineers would check each day and then pay the laborers personally every two weeks for their work. That direct implementation of projects was not something I was used to doing, but it was much cheaper and allowed us to keep control of the project.

The second problem was that we did not know where the best locations were to build micro-hydros. We decided to focus on a few key districts that had been neglected by most and work with those district councils to find the best locations. The first call I made was to my old friend Yasir in Darai Nur. He knew the district well, and since we had already built a micro-hydro together on his land years before he knew what I was looking for. We met with the district council, and they told me it was fine to work with Yasir to talk to the villages and find the best sites.

Hanging Out at Yasir's House in Darai Nur

One of the places that everyone talked about was at the top of the mountain in Darai Nur in a small village that was virtually cut off from civilization. Lak, Hadi, and I decided to go and check the place out. The road ended halfway up the mountain, and the rest of the way we had to go on foot. When we parked our trucks at the end of the road, the villagers said it was only a short walk up, so I brought one bottle of water, and we began our hike. As I walked up the mountain it was like entering another world. Women were working in the fields with beautiful pastel dresses, and the men wore heavy eyeliner makeup on their eyes and put colorful flowers in their hats. The villagers all had the Pashai facial features, with blonde hair and blue eyes. It was as though a tiny bit of Western genes had been transplanted on top of that cut-off mountain village. The hike up the mountain was not the short walk I was promised. It took hours before we reached the top, and by then I was so thirsty that I would have drunk a glass of mud. At the top was a young man with a metal cup of water that he offered me to drink. I figured water from the top of the mountain must be clean, so I gulped it down without hesitation. I would pay for that later with a nasty stomach parasite.

The villagers were amazed to see a Westerner in their village for the first time ever. They made us a great lunch, and we sat down to talk about the micro-hydro site. The villagers took us on another hike further up the mountain to the site where a small micro-hydro had been constructed many years ago, but it was kind of a homemade contraption that had broken down and needed complete reconstruction. As much as I would have loved to build a system up there, getting the equipment and personnel there to do it was too much of a problem. We ended up having to decline that area, but the experience of seeing the village and meeting the people there was awesome. We ended up working with the district council to find two alternative sites in Darai Nur, where we were able to build the first two successful micro-hydro projects.

It was important to us that we kept as much money in the local economy as possible. In Jalalabad, there happened to be a metal working shop that had experience building turbines for micro-hydros. A turbine is the part that is in contact with the water and uses the pressure of the water to spin. I was skeptical that a local shop could build such a technical device and had to see it for myself. Lak, Hadi, and I drove over to the shop and met the owner. It was a small, dirty shop that was full of grease and flying sparks as workers were rebuilding drive shafts and all kinds of parts for cars. We were led to the back of the shop, where the owner showed us a turbine wheel he had just finished for a different program. I inspected the turbine and was impressed by the workmanship. The engineers said the guy's turbines were just what they needed to get the job done. Other local vendors sold to us the cement, generators, and wire that we needed. We were ready to start work.

As primitive as some of the villages appeared, I was pleasantly surprised by the ingenuity and construction abilities of the local villagers. They gathered large stones, sand, and aggregate from the riverbeds to mix with the cement that we provided to build the reservoir and small power room. That saved a ton of money and allowed us to build full micro-hydro systems at a quarter of the cost that other programs could. Not having to pay a general contractor was another added benefit to our savings. The most important thing, though, was not about financial savings. More important was that the villagers were building their own project, on their own terms, where they wanted it, and how they wanted it. They got to choose who would work on the project. They got to choose where it was located, and they got to choose how the power was distributed. It was an excellent lesson in local democracy and helped the village come together to complete a common goal. That lesson stuck in my head and was useful in future projects.

Not all micro-hydro projects went well. Sometimes there was infighting between villages that caused projects to be delayed or canceled if a consensus could not be reached. In the district of Kot, we attempted to build a system in the district council's chosen village, where there was a perfect spot for a micro-hydro system. The power from that system would have provided electricity to two neighboring villages. Unfortunately, just prior to construction one village raised complaints, so we conducted a shura (meeting) to iron out the issues. I thought the villagers were complaining that they were going to be left with less power than the other village, and I wanted to ensure that that would not be the case. Instead, the complaint was that they did not want the neighboring village to have any power at all because they had some personal issues between them. After an hour of negotiations, it was clear that the problem would not be solved. We ended up canceling the project altogether. I was disappointed that we spent so much time trying to help those villagers, who ended up not receiving any benefit from the project themselves just to screw over their neighbors.

Through the year that I spent building micro-hydros, we ended up building about 16 systems that provided power for lights, cell phone charging, and small electronics. It was a huge benefit to villages that had little access to reliable power in the past. The biggest hurdle was maintenance and proper operation of the systems, which became a huge problem. Even though the program included training for operations and maintenance, many of the villagers did not take that seriously. They knew they were only supposed to use lights and small electronics that would not take much power load. Instead, many plugged in heaters or stoves or other high-load items, causing problems for the system. Generators and control systems had to be reinstalled often due to that issue, however, some villages did not want to pay for the problems they caused, and systems would lay unused. That kind of problem was the reason I had wanted to work on irrigation systems in the first place. Although we did not end up building as many systems as I would have liked, the biggest benefit that we provided was a complete list and map of every viable micro-hydro location in all districts of the Nangarhar Province. That would allow anyone else who wanted to build those systems to know where the best sites were and how much power capacity each site could provide. The engineers worked tirelessly with the villagers for hundreds of hours to complete that work, and I appreciated their efforts.

Other Aid Agencies

There were so many aid agencies working on a multitude of problems throughout the province. It would be impossible to name them all, but a few notable programs taught lessons to me for good or bad. The expats from those programs all became good friends, and we enjoyed our time working to solve problems in one of the most challenging places imaginable. One program was run by a great group of mostly Americans that really wanted to make a difference in the lives of farmers. The head of the program, Johan, was a seasoned veteran of fighting poppy in multiple countries and had a heart as big as his brain. The group ran a large agriculture program that worked on rebuilding irrigation systems, helping farmers switch to other crops, and then bringing those crops to market. It was arguably the most beneficial program that USAID sponsored in Nangarhar. The only problem was that the program was only funded to provide about 10 percent of what was actually needed to produce long-lasting results.

Another great program was working in only two of the 22 districts in Nangarhar, but its work was significant. That group worked with nearly every farmer to provide an alternative to poppy growth. The farmers got to choose from a poultry program, an orchard-growing program, or were given all of the seed and knowhow to grow a vegetable plot that would provide the family with all of the vegetables they needed for the season. They also worked with villages to build mini-silos to effectively store enough wheat for the year for the family. It was very successful, because it was comprehensive and ensured that every farmer was affected and included. Lak, Hadi, and I went on multiple field missions with Dr. Arif, who led the program. We had lunch out in the field with the villagers, and I could tell that the poultry program was working because it was the best chicken I had ever tasted.

Learning About Mini-silos in a Rural Village

Although nearly all aid agencies and programs had the best of intentions and tried hard to make a difference, there were others that were looking to take advantage of the situation for either profit or name recognition, regardless of the consequences. Billions of dollars of aid was spent in Afghanistan, and much of that amount was wasted. Some of it was due to corruption, and some of it was due to incompetence. It always pissed me off when I would hear Americans say that corruption was just "part of the cost of doing business in Afghanistan!" That was a justification that I could not accept. I am sure that there was some level of corruption and waste in some of the projects that I ran, but I would never be okay with that and always looked to stop it anywhere that I could and punish those who had taken part.

How Project Corruption Often Happened

Here is a good real-world example of how traditional contracted projects would have corruption and waste problems versus a directly implemented project conducted the way that my team worked. That case involved two identical micro-hydros built very near each other in Nangarhar. With a contracted project, the sponsor would take the specifications for the project and put the project out for bid. Several vendors would then bid on the project, and normally the lowest bid would win. Many of the bidding processes were corrupt, where bidders would get together and drive up the price to make it more expensive and then each take a cut of the project. Other times members of the sponsor organization who chose the winning bid were also in on the graft and would receive kickbacks from the winning bidder.

Once construction was underway, the leaders in the community would see that the contractor was making a huge sum of money on the project, and then those leaders would shake down the contractor for a cut of the money or create problems for him. Also, in some areas there were Taliban and other insurgents who would shake down the contractor for money, or they would attack the contractor's equipment or personnel. Since the contractor needed to complete the work in order to be paid, he was forced to spend a large amount of his profit on paying off all of those parties. That would drive that particular micro-hydro project to cost about $130,000. There was also no transparency since the contractor had no obligation to show where he spent his money on the project. And if there were any changes needed on the project's specifications the contractor could come back and ask for more money from the sponsor, causing prices to rise even more.

When constructing an identical micro-hydro project in the same area using direct implementation, many of those issues were mitigated. First, there was no bidding process for a general contractor, so the corruption in that process was negated. Second, since there was no profit to a contractor there was nothing for the village leaders or Taliban to try to take. The only money spent out in the field was to pay the laborers directly into their hands. If the Taliban or village leaders wanted to try to steal the few dollars out of the hands of villagers, they would face serious backlash from them.

The materials were purchased from local vendors at the lowest price, and although the person purchasing the materials may try to run a scam with vendors to inflate the prices that was mitigated, since we already knew how much the materials would generally cost, and any significant deviation from those costs was easily identified. We also hired monitors, whose entire job was to watch for those corrupt practices and report directly to the program manager. Conducting the same micro-hydro project in that way would cost approximately $30,000. There was full transparency with the process, and we were willing to open our books to anyone who wanted to see them to show where every dollar was spent. There was also complete flexibility, so if any issues came up we would make changes without any penalty, and if villagers created any problems we would simply shut the project down. As you can see, it cost 75 percent less to implement projects through direct implementation. It was more challenging to do it that way, but with proper systems in place it was still rather easy.

"60 Minutes" Showcase

Our work on micro-hydros became a hit. One day the U.S. State Department representative for our program called me and said the iconic TV program "60 Minutes" was coming to Afghanistan to do a story on our efforts to stop poppy cultivation. They wanted to showcase our micro-hydros as a successful reward program that was incentivizing villages to stop poppy cultivation. Although I would say that our efforts were nice, they were certainly not helping that many farmers due to the small scale of the program. It did help some businesses and hundreds of individuals but was a far cry from the serious development needed to change anything in the long run.

I had never been on prime-time TV before, so that was pretty exciting. Lara Logan and a couple of the producers were being flown into Nangarhar in an old Russian helicopter and would land in Darai Nur near one of our micro-hydro sites. The hardest part was finding a flat place to land, since Darai Nur is mostly made up of steep mountains. The farmers created little terraces to plant their crops down the mountainside, so finding a suitable terrace close to the micro-hydro site was a challenge. We did end up finding a decent terrace just big enough to land. The Ukrainian pilots were known for their skills and risk-taking with those choppers, and in the end the helicopter landed without too much trouble. The villagers all came out to see the spectacle. It was the first time a Russian-made helicopter had landed in Darai Nur since the Soviet invasion, so it may have looked a bit crazy.

The famous host Lara Logan and some other gentlemen from the U.S. State Department popped out of the helicopter, and we were there to meet them. We took them around the micro-hydro site, and I had the engineers show them how it operated. The engineers were proud and anxious to show everyone their great work. The visitors were very impressed with the engineering and workmanship created by those villagers in the middle of nowhere on top of a mountain. The system was working well and was providing power to two of the largest villages in Darai Nur. Lara Logan and her entourage were talking to the villagers about poppy cultivation and why they had stopped growing it. The villagers talked about the assistance they had been given with electricity and how the government had enforced the ban. They were proud of the system they had built and asked that projects like that would continue in their villages, since there was so much need. It was a good visit. Months later the show aired, and I started getting Facebook messages from friends like, "Dude, I was just switching through the channels and suddenly there you were on '60 Minutes'! What the hell are you doing over there again?" It was always hard to describe my job to anyone not familiar with Afghanistan, which was virtually everyone I knew.

Our Micro-hydro Turbine in Darai Nur

Marines Shooting Incident

The years 2007 to 2008 were relatively prosperous in Nangarhar, and security incidents were down. It seemed that the province was on the right track in many ways. But one particular incident seemed to make that situation reverse. In 2007, a Marines Special Operations unit was attacked by a car bomb and reported ambush. During the attack, the Marines reportedly returned fire, and several innocent civilians were reported to have been killed by the Marines during the attack and their escape from the ambush. Differing reports and investigations made it difficult to tell exactly what had happened, but the damage to the military's reputation and respect in Nangarhar was certainly shaken. It would have been easy to see how insurgents could have used that incident to incite hatred for the foreigners in their country and to recruit fighters to exact revenge. Even though apologies were made, and reparations were eventually given, there was a palpable change in the attitudes of Afghans that was easy to feel.

Blowing Up Cars

Later in 2008 there was an IED attack on a U.S. Army vehicle in the city of Jalalabad. That was not a very common occurrence. The bomb was so massive that it flipped over one of the armored Humvees. Apparently it was a car bomb. Worried that other cars in the immediate area may also contain explosives, the U.S. Army unit destroyed several cars around the site just to make sure. One of those cars happened to belong to one of my guards. That guy's entire job was to keep me safe, and suddenly the U.S. military had destroyed his car that was parked on the street while he was shopping. The guard asked me to intervene at the PRT to see what I could do to make up for his destroyed car. Being the former Civil Affairs team leader there I knew that they could pay reparations to him for destroying his car. There was a fund specifically for that purpose. I understood why they had done it, but when you destroy an innocent guy's car in Afghanistan you better make up for it.

I went to the PRT and talked to the major in charge of Civil Affairs. He told me he would look into the issue, but he did not seem very enthused about it. Months went by with no answer. I asked him again if there was any movement on the issue. I knew it was really just a matter of doing some paperwork. He told me that he was still looking into it. I was disappointed, since I knew what that really meant was that he was not doing a damn thing about it. After more time went by and the PRT unit was getting ready to change over, I knew that if we did not get some resolution the issue would be lost when the units changed, like everything else. The final time I approached him he told me that there would be no compensation because the vehicles were illegally parked. I snickered, as there was really no such thing in Jalalabad. People parked wherever they could or wanted. It was really just an excuse by him, or someone higher ranking, to do nothing about the issue. That blew my mind because my guard was one of many who lost their cars that day. By not compensating them, it just added another rift between the U.S. military and the Afghan citizens. Afghans do not make a lot of money, and those cars would be very valuable to them, some worth years of their wages.

Wheat Distribution Issues

One of the ways the U.S. government tried to help farmers was by distributing wheat seed to them to grow instead of poppy. Although growing wheat would never fetch enough profit to offset the money that could be gained from growing poppy, giving away wheat seed for free could help take a bit of the sting out of it for the farmers. Unfortunately, nearly every wheat seed distribution that I witnessed was a mess. The seed almost always came late to the province. Wheat seed must be in the ground by a certain time of the season in order to grow enough to get a decent yield. Seed that arrived too late could not be planted. In order to distribute the seed, farmers would be given vouchers that they could redeem for bags of seed at a distribution point. There were rumors of people simply selling their vouchers or selling the seed as soon as they got it. After all, there may have been a more dire need than wheat seed, so it could act as a bargaining chip. Others simply stored the seed or milled it to get flour for bread. That was a shame, since if the seed was planted in time it would yield far more flour at harvest. Whatever the reason, it was sad that we could not get our act together enough to make those distributions fully useful.

Partying with Friends

Since I was no longer a Soldier I was able to partake in all of the fun that expats had in the province. That mostly consisted of partying at the one big expat hangout, the Taj. Thursday nights were party nights, since the Muslim holy day was Friday, and no one had to work. Some of the guys who ran the Taj smuggled beer out of Kabul and drove it down to Jalalabad to stock the tiki bar and keep us all drunk during our time there. The Taj also had a large swimming pool that we used for sunbathing, swimming, and falling into late at night. We met others who would become lifelong friends, talked about the things we were doing, and had a great break from work. It was a little Western oasis in the middle of an otherwise hostile place. There were often worries that the place was being targeted by insurgents, since everyone, including Afghan locals, knew about it. We joked that attacking that house would be a big mistake by the insurgents, because there were more guns and experienced fighters among us there than any attacking force could throw at us. Luckily we never had to put that to the test.

Tuesday night was also another fun night. Many of us got together to play poker at one of the USAID program's guesthouses. I am pretty sure that I never won much, but we had a great time and made a ton of friends. When one group of friends left the country for other jobs, they were replaced with other people, and the cycle repeated. International development folks tend to be friendly, open minded, and just plain fun. We were all there to make a difference and shared common values. It was a good group of people that I will always remember.

One particular conversation that I remember having was with Johan. We were both pretty drunk, and I was talking to him about my ideas on comprehensive development of irrigation systems. I told him, "What if we went district by district and rebuilt all the irrigation systems at once, hiring thousands of people and then in the end they would have all the water they need?" He slowly turned his head and replied, "That would really be cool!" "Well, I'm gonna do it man," I said drunkenly slurring my words. I had no way of backing that up at the time, but soon I would have the opportunity.

CHAPTER 3. TRANSITION TO AID WORK

As my two years working for the counternarcotics program were nearly up I started looking at where I wanted to go from there. One of my friends, Tom, who ran the Taj, was working for a small program that was doing projects in the same direct implementation method that I was building micro-hydros. He told me that that small program was going to be expanding, since they had been having good success. The whole aim of the program was to get people employed, so that they could have enough money to get through the tough winter months. The program was only operating in a few large cities, and mostly was paying people to clean up the streets and gutters and fix emergency problems. He told me that the program was expanding into the rural areas of 12 provinces, and that they needed guys like me who had experience doing those kinds of projects in the rural areas. He was leaving the job and wondered if I could possibly take over for him in Nangarhar. I was immediately interested. He told me that his boss was going to be coming to stay at the Taj for a few nights and that I should meet him.

Meeting the New Boss

The next Friday I went to the Taj for a little daytime drinking and relaxing in the pool for the day, and there I met Stan, the owner of CAC, the small development company that Tom was telling me about. Stan was a stout, bald man who looked like someone you would not want to cross at the bar. After a few beers, it ended up being just Stan and me swimming in the pool talking. Stan asked me what I was working on, and I told him about our direct implementation micro-hydro projects and how I would really like to take the lessons from that and expand into doing irrigation systems. I told him that there were about 1,500 irrigation systems in Nangarhar alone and how the vast majority of systems were in a sad state of disrepair.

He told me about their program and how the idea was to put as many people to work as possible. So he asked me, "If you had $2 million dollars to work with, what would you do?" I said, "I'll tell you what I would do: I would go district by district, building out the entire irrigation infrastructure at one time, hiring thousands of people and at the end leave the district with a completely working irrigation infrastructure that would seriously benefit farmer yields for years to come." Stan was very knowledgeable about agriculture, having worked with farmers for years in southern Afghanistan during the Taliban's reign and afterward. He was one of the only Westerners that I knew who worked in Afghanistan with the Taliban. No one knew southern Afghanistan better than Stan, but he did not know much about eastern Afghanistan, which was a very different place.

Stan and I continued to talk over some beers, and he told me that he was going to need someone to take over the eastern region, which included the Nangahar, Kunar, and eventually Laghman provinces. The small office and handful of local Afghans they currently had was only for working in the city of Jalalabad, so he really needed someone who knew the outer districts well and could build a large team and a new program quickly. He said that I would have complete authority to run the program with little interference, and he liked my massive irrigation program ideas. It was strange to have a job interview take place in a pool and tiki bar over beers, but that was pretty much what happened. Shortly afterward I received my new contract and was ready to move to the new role. I did not have to go far, since the new office was just down the road from my old hangout at the governor's compound. I was happy to be moving from the shipping container I had resided in for two years to a nice, large house on the outskirts of Jalalabad.

Making the Move

As I was moving to the new job in the fall of 2009 I decided to take a little vacation in between jobs to clear my head a little and get refreshed before taking on the stress of building a whole new program. The task in front of me was a daunting one. Before going on vacation, I moved all of my belongings from my shipping container over to the new office and house that I was going to be living in. That gave me a chance to catch up with Tom before he left the program and meet some of the new staff that I would be working with. Since I was going to be the new regional manager taking over for Tom, he introduced me to the operations manager, a young Afghan named Wadi, who basically had been Tom's right-hand man.

The minute that I met Wadi I knew something was wrong. We introduced ourselves, and Wadi started telling me how he had already made great plans for the upcoming year. His plan was to basically become a sanitation department for the cities of Jalalabad and Asadabad, the capital of Kunar. He had planned to purchase a fleet of garbage trucks, and it appeared that the entire program that he had envisioned was going to consist of cleaning out gutters and taking away trash. He was well acquainted with the mayors and was determined that that was going to be the plan going forward. I told him that we might do that kind of work on a small scale but that irrigation in the rural districts was going to be our main focus. I was taken aback a bit when he quickly protested saying, "No, the projects have to be labor intensive, so you can't do that! We are going to do this work with the mayors that I already have planned!" It was clear that there was some nefarious interest that he had in those projects. He was used to getting his way with Tom who gave him very little oversight. I sternly told him, "I'm not sure you understand our relationship. I will direct the program when I start work next month. You guys can continue the small-scale cleanup projects until I get settled, but then we are going to refocus. I will bring in the team to do it." I could tell he was mad and was hiding something. All I knew was that that guy had some kind of corruption scam going, and I was not going to run a program that would tolerate it. Tom warned me that something was up with Wadi and thought that he should be removed, but also that Stan really liked him, so I would have to tolerate him.

Heading to Singapore

After a couple of weeks relaxing in Europe, I needed to go to the company's headquarters in Singapore to do my contract paperwork and introduction to the company. It was my first time there, and I was amazed by the place. It was so beautiful and green, yet a bustling metropolis. Of course, years of dirty, dry Afghanistan may have made Singapore look even nicer. The 20-hour flight to get there was well worth it. The company had me picked up at the airport and taken to a swanky hotel called the Quincy. Treated to a five-star welcome, I felt like a superstar. I walked to the office in the morning, and met the headquarters' staff and Rani, Stan's wife and co-owner of the company.

After getting a briefing from the HR staff and completing my contract paperwork, I sat down with Rani for a talk. She coyly said, "Well, Chris, in Nangarhar where you are taking over there is this guy Wadi, who is kind of a pain." I said, "Yes, I have met him, and I think I am going to fire him because he is bad news." She sighed in relief and said, "Oh, thank God," as though I had just taken a big weight off of her shoulders. Apparently I was not the only one who felt that way about him. I could tell that Rani was a very intelligent and overall great person. It made me want to do my best for the company. After spending the remainder of the day in Singapore, it was time to fly back to Afghanistan and get started.

Meeting the Leadership in Kandahar

After the long flight to the city of Kandahar, Afghanistan, I was met by a group of Canadian ex- Soldiers, who were also former Civil Affairs operators. They ran the Kandahar Province office in the southern part of the country, and CAC's country office was situated there. That was different from every other development company that all had their offices in Kabul, the capital. I liked that latter setup, because it meant that the country's leadership team was operating right in the thick of the work, keeping it more in touch with the operations on the ground instead of just barking orders from hundreds of miles away in Kabul. As we got ready to leave the airport to go the office the guys handed a pistol to me and had me put on some Afghan local clothes, hat, and a scarf to cover my face. Kandahar was a much more dangerous place than Nangarhar. Instead of armored SUVs that stuck out and screamed "Westerner inside!" we drove unremarkable Toyota Corollas and beat-up trucks that any local Afghan, or insurgent, would not think twice about.

The long drive through town proved to me how different southern Afghanistan was from the northern areas. There were very few smiles on faces, and unlike the optimism happening in Nangarhar it seemed like every person I saw was mad. I was happy to just make it to the compound without any incident. As we rolled up to the gate our guards met us to do a quick check of our vehicles and then waved us in. The guards were handpicked by the local staff that CAC had there for years, so that they could be trusted. I was led into the house and put in a makeshift room, where several beds were lined up and separated by curtains for a little bit of privacy. Since the program was expanding from doing work in about five cities with small offices to 12 full provincial offices there were so many people coming into the country that it was overwhelming the Kandahar office.

After a quick meal, I was introduced to the rest of the country staff. I met Jim, who was the senior program manager for the entire country. He was a former Canadian Soldier who had been stationed in Kandahar Province, and the rest of his staff were other Canadian guys that he had brought in who had served with him there. The vast majority of provincial and regional managers were ex-military like me. I liked that, since it meant that it was a group that was used to less talk and more action. Those guys knew how to operate in dangerous places and get the job done without excuses. The guys in Kandahar were all good friends, and they liked playing tricks on each other, and getting drunk and having bonfires on the roof. Kandahar did not have a great place for expats to go and blow off steam, like the Taj in Nangarhar, so that was the best they could do.

Stan happened to be visiting the country, as well, so after things settled down I sat down to have a meeting with Stan and Jim to discuss the plans for Nangarhar over the next year. Surprisingly, one of the first things that Stan told me was, "Look, you can't fire Wadi. He is important to me." Apparently, Rani had told him about our little talk in Singapore. I told him, "I want to run a straight ship, and he does not seem to want to get on board with my ideas. I want to bring in my own team to run Nangarhar, but how about I have him be the operations officer just for Kunar." Stan agreed, as long as I kept him employed. Jim just kind of went along with the conversation, knowing there was nothing he could say to Stan about Wadi, and he understandably did not want to rock the boat with the boss. I went on to brief Stan and Jim on my comprehensive irrigation plan, and they just nodded and basically said that I could do whatever I wanted. It was good to have the trust and ability to finally run the program I had wanted to run for years.

Finally Back Home in Nangarhar

The next day I caught a flight to Nangarhar and was picked up at the airport/military base by Tom. Unlike the counternarcotics program, we did not really have drivers; we just jumped in our crappy cars and drove ourselves wherever we needed to go. It was wild driving around Afghanistan by myself, where there were essentially no driving rules to speak of. We arrived at what would be my new home for the year. It was a very nice three-story house/office on the outskirts of town. Hundreds of those huge homes — jokingly called "poppy palaces," alluding to the source of money used to construct the elaborate houses — had been built throughout the city. Being the only expat at the time, I took one of two rooms on the third floor, which could only be accessed by a single door on the roof. It was the safest place to be in case of an attack, and I stationed plenty of weapons and ammunition there in case it became an Alamo for us if everything went bad.

I finally got to settle in after running all over the world for a while, and I wasted no time. Tom introduced me to the staff to get started. He said he would stay for a week or so to get me situated, and then he would be moving back to the Taj to live and work there as a security team leader. Tom showed me how project proposals were done, how the finances were handled, and basic staff processes. Although the house was well apportioned, the worst part was the food. We had a local cook, who was, of course, Wadi's cousin. Meals were horrible, and pretty much every meal consisted of the same oily pan-fried chicken with some vegetables. I rarely ate the seemingly inedible food, and usually ended up going to the Army base every day to try and scare up a decent meal. I lost a ton of weight and was pretty unhealthy. Other than that, life at the house was fairly lonely, but I was focused on work anyway, and our weekly expat poker games on Tuesdays and Taj parties on Thursdays kept my morale up.

Fighting Internal Corruption

The biggest concern that I had right from the start was finances. There were actually very few rules when it came to spending money. Along with me, CAC sent a new finance officer, a Filipino national, whom I nicknamed Mayo. He was a great guy and very well versed on financial systems. He was sent there because the company was concerned about the finances in Nangarhar and wanted to make sure everything was on the up and up. It was not, and it did not take Mayo and me very long to figure that out. Wadi had essentially taken over the procurement system, like a mafia boss, so that if anyone needed anything they had to go to him for permission. He would then expect me to rubber stamp each transaction for approval. When I began to scrutinize questionable transactions, Wadi would get angry. I guess Tom let him do whatever he wanted to, since Tom knew that Stan would never fire Wadi anyway.

Throughout my first month there, I was not sure that I was going to stick around. Wadi and I shared an office, and every time I instructed him to do something or stopped him from doing something that he wanted he would immediately send a Skype message to Stan in Singapore. Stan would instantaneously message me to see what the problem was. It was getting stupid, and I was quickly getting tired of it. I could tell that nearly every transaction, from fuel to food, had some kind of money skimming associated with it. Wadi also owned all of the vehicles that he leased to the company at a nice profit. He was a walking conflict of interest. Mayo and I began to put procurement systems in place that would stop those little scams. Wadi was not happy about it, and he fought our efforts for transparency everywhere that he could. The entire staff was handpicked by him, and they were all threatened that they would lose their jobs if they exposed him. There was not much that I could do to remove him, but at least I did what I could to ensure that he did not ruin the program with corruption.

About a month into my job, the USAID representative from Kabul, Farooq, who was in charge of the program, called me and said that he was coming to Nangarhar for a visit. He was an Afghan gentleman from the city of Kandahar who was well educated and had himself designed that program. He suspected that there was corruption happening between Wadi and the mayor's office, but he did not tell me anything about it. I was happy to have him come down. Jim flew up from Kandahar, as well, to meet up with Farooq and check on how I was doing. It ended up being a wild week.

Farooq showed up at the house, and it was the first time that I had met him. I briefed him on my plans for the region, and he was happy to see how ambitious we were going to be with his program. He said that he was only going to be there for the day and wanted to go down to the mayor's office with Wadi. I told him that I would like to go, as well, but he instructed me to stay at my office until he got back. That was pretty weird to me. Why would he not want the manager at the meeting?

When Farooq returned after some time, he finally sat down and had a one-on-one talk with me. He said, "I know there are some serious problems going on here, but you have to do some things to change it." I said, "Okay, what do you want me to do?" He said, "The first thing you need to do is fire the logistics officer who does your procurements." I thought it was a strange move, but he was the guy whom we all ultimately answered to, so if he told us that we needed to do that it must have been pretty important. I felt bad about it, since the logistics guy seemed like a good man, and he really had no choice but to do what Wadi wanted or he would be fired, and he needed the job to support his family. Jim and I called him into the office and let him know that he was being let go. He asked me why, and I told him that I was instructed to do it and had no choice. I told him that I would give him a good recommendation for another job somewhere else. He started crying and said, "If you let me stay, I will tell you everything that is going on here." I hesitated and told him to leave the room. I told Jim, "Hey, that sounds good, and we can get to the bottom of this." Jim said, "Dude I don't want to know." That surprised me for a minute, but I understood that it meant we were going to have a mess to clean up and would have a lot of drama involving Wadi, for sure.

Farooq was very smart about what he was doing. He knew that bringing in a new logistics officer of my choice, who had no relation to Wadi, would expose what had been happening or at least prevent Wadi from exerting pressure on him to have him fired, since I would have his back. As soon as Wadi found out about the firing, he came to me and protested. I told him that it was out of my hands, as it was. Wadi immediately said, "I don't like what is going on here, and I don't think I want to stay any longer. I'm resigning." I wanted to jump up and shout, "Yes!" but kept cool as Jim told him, "You know you don't have to go." I wanted to punch Jim and tell him to shut up. I was finally going to be free of that corrupt pest! Wadi left the next day, and many of his handpicked guys were either fired or quit shortly thereafter. The time had come when I would be able to implement systems to ensure that we could run a clean program that we could be proud of. If Wadi had not left, the program would have been stained with graft.

When Wadi and his gang were finally gone, the remaining guys told me all about the corruption and issues they had with him. They said that they had been threatened that they would be fired if they ever argued with him and knew that due to his relationship with Stan that he could make good on that threat. I later found out that Wadi had doctored invoices where materials for projects were supposedly purchased, but in actuality they simply transferred materials from a former project, and Wadi pocketed the money from that doctored invoice. At one of his houses, we found project materials and machinery that he had taken after the completion of a project. He had apparently used his corruption schemes to purchase land and build properties to enrich himself. His departure was a welcome relief and allowed us to create a very transparent program that we could be proud of.

Building a New Team

I was then able to start building a team to implement my vision. Since the counternarcotics team was starting to throttle down its program, I knew that I could bring on the same group of guys to be the core of our new team. They all knew my vision, since I had been filling their heads with it over the last two years, and they were all very motivated to implement it. Since we were able to work in a nearly identical system as when we built the micro-hydros, directly implementing projects with no contractors, we already knew the basics of how we were going to operate. My former interpreter became the Nangarhar operations manager. The former office manager became deputy provincial manager. The engineers who had built the micro-hydros were now designing our irrigation systems. Other guys from the former counternarcotics team became the new logistics officer and field monitor. We then had a solid team of clean professionals, who I knew were not involved in corruption and were proud to work in an environment where corruption would not be tolerated, and they would be a doing a lot of good work for their own province.

Preparing the Plan

Once the team was in place, we focused on planning our program for the year. We first met with the USAID representatives, who wanted us to focus our irrigation plans on the Rodat, Deh Bala, and Kot districts in the Nangarhar Province, and the Khas Kunar and Asmar districts in the Kunar Province. We still continued our small cleanup projects in the cities of Jalalabad and Asadabad, but they were only a tiny part of our portfolio. We also wanted to do something special for women, who were mostly marginalized. We decided to focus our female-related efforts on rebuilding girls' schools using female workers. Females doing labor was largely unheard of, and most programs focused their women's projects on training to do things that could be accomplished in the home, like sewing, beekeeping, vegetable gardening, and other stay-at-home functions. We took a different approach and had women trained to do basic construction activities, like carpentry, plastering and painting, roof reconstruction, and other nontraditional roles. The women were guarded and worked inside the walls of school compounds so that they would not be bothered, and we had skilled tradesmen overseeing their work. All other projects that we did employed only men in the villages.

After getting our plans approved by USAID, we next met with the provincial leadership to get our plans approved. The director of Women's Affairs happily approved our women's projects and helped to organize the female laborers. The director of irrigation also quickly approved our irrigation strategy, although he thought that we were overly ambitious to try to build out a whole district's irrigation infrastructure at one time. He showed us his "maps" of the irrigation systems in the districts that he had, but they were basically just rudimentary sketches of the district with no scale or actual location of systems. All it really gave us was the number of systems in each district, and that was good enough to start. It did surprise me to have a director of irrigation who did not actually know where any of the irrigation systems were. He had enough staff to find that out, but they were too lazy to bother doing any real work.

The last thing that we needed to do in order to start working in the districts was to get with all of the other aid agencies to find out where they were working so we did not overlap and plan to work on the same systems. There were several programs that were doing a couple of irrigation projects in each district, like Johan's program, so we went to each agency to get all of the information that we could. Most aid agencies were happy to coordinate with us and shared their data willingly, but others were not as helpful. We did the best that we could to ensure that we were ready to go.

Rodat

The first district that we focused on was Rodat. The district was relatively close to the city of Jalalabad and was a perfect place to test our surge of irrigation projects. We called a shura with the district leadership, which included the elders of all villages and the district council. A couple of hundred people showed up to listen to us lay out our plans. I asked the director of irrigation to come along so that he could lay the groundwork with the elders. He introduced me and let me talk. I started by telling them that we wanted to first work with the village leaders to identify all of the irrigation systems in the district, and then create a plan to fix all of the major systems at one time. It took a second for everyone to absorb what I was telling them. It was a huge undertaking, and many of the elders had heard lavish speeches before but with little action actually taking place. I introduced the engineering team to the elders, and said that the engineers would go out with the elders and inspect every system, determine what needed to be fixed, and then we would meet up again in two weeks to discuss implementing the plan. The elders all agreed, and we signed a memorandum of understanding to do the work.

After two weeks, the engineers had worked their butts off in the field and in the office to see all of the 36 individual systems and had come up with engineering specs for fixing all of them that needed work. In Nangarhar, there were two different types of irrigation systems: intake and karez. Intake systems were simply diversion dams that took water out of a stream and directed the water into a canal system. Karezes were interesting tunnel systems, where someone would identify an underground reservoir and then dig a tunnel system to access the hidden reservoir. Some of those tunnels were miles long. All of the 36 systems were in a horrible state of disrepair, and some were barely useable after 30 years of war and neglect. Our goal was to permanently fix those systems, so that the farmers would always have access to water for their crops.

We called a second shura and met with the elders once more. That time we had a full plan ready to implement. We planned to hire about 2,500 people to work on the projects. Each irrigation project would have a local foreman chosen from the village, who would be in charge of the work. That gave the village ownership of its own project. We would provide all of the engineering oversight, materials, and payment to the workers. We expected the total cost of all 36 systems to be around $800,000 and it would take 100 days. At the time, our rate for paying laborers was the equivalent of U.S. $4 per day. Although that seems insane by Western standards, it was actually much higher than the average U.S. $2 to $3 a day that a normal laborer would make. Since there was little to no work out in the districts, it was a great opportunity for them. The elders seemed amazed that we were able to put a plan together so soon and that we were actually serious about executing the projects. The elders quickly got to work choosing foremen and laborers for the projects. Within a week, we had acquired thousands of bags of cement, hundreds of shovels, pickaxes, wheelbarrows, and other materials and were ready to put shovels in the ground.

With just over three months from start to finish for the Rodat projects, it was very important that everything went smoothly with few issues. But that was wishful thinking in a place like Afghanistan. Infighting between elders, villages, and government officials was a burden. Those villages were not used to projects without contractors to scam or pilfer for profit. Some of the elders were sure that there would be some way to profit off of such a huge program. When they could not really find a way to scam the program, they would levy baseless complaints or try to stop projects, hoping that they could get a payoff for doing so. Of course, no one will actually come out and say, "Hey, give me money, or I will create problems for you!" They would simply stop the project and hope that we would have to bow to their wishes like others had before. No such luck for them.

We handled every issue the same way. If there was a problem, we would send out a delegation to meet with the elders, identify the issue, and work out a solution in their own customary way. That required patience; something that I am not known for. If there was a reasonable explanation for the stoppage, we would adjust as needed. Our program had no contractors, so we had the ability to change anything that we wanted within reason. Sometimes an irrigation system was designed in such a way that disadvantaged a farmer that we did not know about. That was not a problem. We could immediately make changes to the design, everyone would be happy, and work could continue. Other times, if the elders were trying to create problems in hope of getting a payoff, we would immediately halt the projects and tell them that we would not continue the project at that site until the interference stopped. Once word got out to the villagers that the project was stopped, along with their paychecks, it did not take long for that pressure to change their behavior. Normally, the elders would fold and come back to us within a day saying, "Never mind, everything is fine. Please start the work again." We would warn them that further interference could lead to canceling the project, and they would have to explain that to their villagers. That was a conversation none of them wanted to have. We had very few issues once everyone understood how serious we were about that.

Organizing and running each site was a work of art that our team had mastered. Every laborer signed in on an attendance sheet each day. Since the vast majority of those men were illiterate and could not write, they showed their attendance by dipping their thumb in ink and putting a thumbprint on the attendance sheet. The literate foreman would help them do that each morning. Without proper monitoring, it would be easy to cheat the system, so we sent out monitors/spies to ensure that the laborers were present. The monitors would go to a site, take pictures of the work, check on quality control, and count laborers to ensure that that number matched the attendance sheet. The monitors carried GPS trackers programmed with their cameras so that we could ensure that they went to the sites and that the pictures that they took matched up with the correct sites. It was a pretty foolproof way to ensure that no one cheated, and we could show complete transparency.

In general, the projects went smoothly. We went on several site visits to see the progress, and I was floored by the efficiency and skill shown by the villagers. The masonry work required to build the intakes and canal systems was a skill that seemed inborn to Afghans. They worked in practical assembly-line order. Dozens of men excavated an area, while a dozen more mixed cement. There would be another group that collected stones, while another group chiseled them to size. A few guys would be in charge of mixing cement, while an army of others formed a wheelbarrow brigade that ferried cement to the masons, who would build the structures. Overseeing the sites were our busy engineers, who would consistently check to ensure that the work was completed on time and correctly. I could not have been prouder of the results. After just over three months of work, the Rodat project was completed, and all 36 irrigation systems were functioning the way that they were supposed to.

In the end, we had hired over 3,700 laborers for the project, each for about 50 days. That was over a thousand more people than we had planned for, because the elders wanted to change out laborers at the halfway point in order to bring in fresh guys and also to ensure that the most people possible benefited from the project. We also came in $170,000 *under* budget, which was strange to see in any government-sponsored project. The project not only employed thousands of people, it also rehabilitated over 4,000 acres of land that were ready to grow any viable crops. The district leadership threw a huge party at the end of the project and thanked us for the great work. I refused to go to the party, as I did not want to be the center of attention at the celebration. The Afghan team members, especially the engineers, deserved all of the praise for the project, and they got it. After the success that we found in Rodat, we were confident that our program could work anywhere.

Kot

It did not take long for word to get around that there was a big program out there that was building irrigation systems, and many districts wanted in on it. But we did have to stick to the districts that we were assigned by USAID at the time, and our next district was Kot. As luck would have it, the new district sub-governor of Kot, Abdul Haq, was an old friend of mine, whom I had met when I was a Civil Affairs officer years before. He was a former Mujahedeen commander, who fought the Soviet Union back in the 1980s and was well respected among his people. He was a gentleman, who was always smiling and happy to see me. I will never forget that the guy had giant hands that would engulf mine anytime a handshake occurred. I always wondered how many Russians those hands had killed. He found out about our project and came to my house for a visit. We drank a gallon of tea and talked about old times for an hour, making the interpreter really earn his pay that day. I told him about our project and how we wanted to start work in his district next. He agreed to get all of the elders together to have a large shura to discuss it.

The next week we drove out to Kot and were greeted by hundreds of elders. The building they chose to have the shura in was not big enough to host the crowd, but they did their best to accommodate everyone. Abdul Haq quieted everyone down and introduced me as his old friend and asked that the elders let me speak. I explained our program to them, and pretty much everyone agreed. There were a couple of older men who started shouting about how many people had come out promising work but never did anything. I understood that that had been a problem and sympathized with them. I told them about the project that we had just completed in Rodat as an example of what we could do. Many of them had friends in Rodat and had heard about the program, so they quickly quieted down the protesting old men. I had learned the lesson years ago that you always let the oldest elders have their say, even if they were just rambling and talking crazy. It was disrespectful to argue and talk down to them, so I let them yell as loudly as they wanted to and answered all of their questions calmly and politely. I did want to get home alive.

Just like in Rodat, we followed the same game plan. The engineers were to go with the elders to identify all of the irrigation systems and create plans to fix them. We then returned to the district leadership with the full plan and got approval to start work. The projects again consisted of intake and karez systems, but there were 43 projects, and they were much bigger and more complicated than the ones we had done in Rodat. After our success completing 36 at a time in Rodat, we figured that we could handle 43 projects simultaneously by adding another engineer. The same processes were followed, so we thought those projects would most likely go as smoothly as the last. That did not turn out to be the case.

Just prior to our work commencing, Kot was hit by a string of bombs. One of the bombs hit a U.S. military convoy, killing two Soldiers. The bomber was apparently a lone-wolf insurgent, who had the audacity to leave notes near the bomb sites saying something like, "You can't catch me!" The PRT leadership was obviously upset, and some wanted me to cancel my program in Kot as punishment. They really had little power to stop me, but I told them that my program might help by getting the community to turn on the bomber. I warned Abdul Haq that any further security issues could lead to cancelation of the projects. I was certainly not going to send my guys to work in the field everyday if they were going to be targeted and harmed. He, along with the other elders, agreed and guaranteed our security. Work commenced, and suddenly 3,800 members of the community were busy working on the 43 irrigation systems. Within a couple of weeks, the bomber was identified and neutralized. I cannot say that it was our project that caused that, but I bet it did not hurt.

Unfortunately, that was not the only problem we had in Kot. The district contained members of two tribes: Shinwari and Mohmand. They did not always see eye to eye and had their own internal politics that could cause problems. Three of the projects had internal issues that slowed down their progress and delayed the work past our deadlines. We had several meetings to get things moving, but our efforts were in vain. After several attempts to get the projects on track, the elders asked us to cancel the three projects. Unfortunately, we did cancel them in the middle of construction. Some people would rather fight than have water. The other 40 projects were completed with minimal disruption, and the projects were hailed as a huge success for the district. In the end, the Kot projects employed 3,800 villagers, rehabilitated about 5,000 acres of land, and cost just over $1 million. That came out to $25,000 per irrigation system, which was a bargain compared to similar projects in the province that were usually completed for four times as much.

Deh Bala and Chaparhar

With two districts successfully completed, we were ready to go to our third and final district for the year, Deh Bala. Since things were going so smoothly that Stan gave me a call and said that he really wanted to do something special by having us simultaneously complete the district of Chaparhar. That was a huge challenge for three reasons. First, time was running out since our program ran in one-year increments. We would complete a year's worth of work and wait until the last month or two to hear if the program would continue. We expected it to but could not count on it, so we had to plan on finishing the projects prior to the stop date, and we had just enough time to complete one more round of projects. Second, although Deh Bala only had 50 irrigation systems to complete, Chaparhar had 80 individual irrigation systems. That meant completing double the amount of work that we had done in Rodat and Kot and doing it quickly. Although I had some serious reservations, I had to do what the boss wanted. The third issue was that Chaparhar was a particularly fragmented district, with a mix of several tribes competing for dominance. That was the place that Bin Laden had one of his houses that was bombed by President Clinton in 1998 after the African Embassy bombings. So we had added security issues to worry about.

We did all of our planning and district meetings as usual, and everything was moving along well. The Chaparhar District meeting was pretty humorous. We already had all of the irrigation systems identified, and I had plotted them using Google Earth as I usually did. When we got to the meeting, one particular elder jumped up and started yelling at me. He said, "You have no idea what you are talking about, and do not even know how many systems we have or where they are located, so you are just lying about being able to do all this work." I quietly took the screaming with a smile as usual and opened my laptop to show him all of the irrigation systems plotted on the satellite image of the districts. The old man had thick glasses on and could barely see, so he walked up to the front of the crowd and looked at the screen. He looked at me with a bewildered smile on his face and went back to his spot and sat down quietly. I then continued to brief them on the plan, and all went well from there.

As we began work on the 130 systems in the two districts, things were running smoothly. We were employing 13,000 people and putting millions of dollars into the local economy that was sorely needed. The cooperation from the elders in the districts was pretty good. We did not have to deal with a lot of work stoppages. I think that word got around that we did not play games and that there was nothing to steal, so people stopped trying. With a lack of issues and things moving along, it seemed that we were going to pull off those projects without all of the worries I had earlier. Boy was I wrong.

While many of the projects were being built, we were hit with massive flooding on a scale that we had not seen before. Since most of the projects were being built on the riverbeds, we used simple cofferdams to divert any trickling water from the area being built. Those floods were torrential, and they did not stop. For months, we were hit by flash flood after flash flood. Several projects were destroyed and had to be rebuilt many times over. That caused our materials costs to rise substantially, and, of course, labor costs went up since we had to redo so much work. That was not a big deal, really, since the whole goal of our program was to get people working. But it was a major cause of stress for my team and me. Many projects had to be put on hold until the rainy season ended, and the waters calmed down. Luckily we did get our extension for the next year, so we had time to finish the projects. In the end, we spent $4.8 million on the two districts; $3 million of that amount went to the 13,000 laborers for a total of about $230 per laborer. That was a lot of money poured into very impoverished districts.

A Completed Intake and Canal System

Mistake in Decorum

Although we had very few problems with the district leadership during the implementation of the projects, we did have one close call that was completely my fault. Most companies working in the provinces hired expensive security companies to guard the Westerners and program staff. CAC did things a little differently. We hired our own internal security guards, who were chosen by our relationships with respected leaders in the province. We trusted those guys with our lives and had to have complete faith that they would fight if needed and protect us in case of an attack on the office or while we were in the field. I liked to go out and periodically check on the projects to ensure that everything was going well.

One day a couple of the managers and I decided to go look at a few of the irrigation projects in Deh Bala. We had the Westerners' car with the head of security, another manager, and me in it, and then three pickup trucks with our security team in them. The security team did not wear uniforms and kind of looked like a ragtag bunch of yahoos, riding in the bed of the pickups with their AK-47s. My mistake was that I should have gone to the district center to inform the sub-governor and police chief that we were looking at the projects. It was a matter of respect, and it let them know that there were good guys in the area and to not worry. Since I did not do that, some of the local villagers called up the police chief and said that there was an armed gang rolling through their villages that they did not recognize. The villagers thought we were Taliban coming to attack villages.

When we reached one of the work sites, I was walking around up on a hill looking at the work when I got a call on my radio from the security manager saying, "Hey, dude, you better get down here, the police are here arresting our guys, and the police chief is pissed!" I quickly went back down the hill, and as I came into sight I could see our security team surrounded by police with rifles, grenade launchers, and all of our guys kneeling on the ground disarmed. I was not sure what the issue was until I got there, but the police chief quickly let me know, saying, "What are you doing here coming to these villages with an armed gang. The villagers called me saying we were under attack!" I put my hand over my heart and told him how sorry I was for not informing him about our presence there. I said, "Please forgive me, I just wanted to check on the projects we are doing with your district. I should have come to see you first. Our team is legal, here is the permission letter we have from Governor Sherzai himself. I am very impressed with how fast you responded to the villagers' calls. You must be a very good police chief!"

My attempt at apologizing and flattering him failed, and he was still pissed. The police chief said that he was taking all of us to jail in the district center and motioned for me to get in his truck. I changed my tactic a little and said, "Sir, I know you are upset, but just consider this for a second. If you take us to the district center, all that is going to happen is that I will talk to the sub-governor, Mr. Rohani, who is a friend of mine, and he is going to just tell you to let us go. We are employing thousands of Deh Bala villagers in our program, and the sub-governor is so happy with our work, he is not going to risk the projects being shut down if we go to jail. So, you can take us there if you feel you have to, but it will really just be a waste of time. Please let us go on our way, and I promise I will ensure we call before coming again." I put my hand out hoping he would shake it and gave him a smile. He finally lightened up and told us we could go. I took a deep breath, and we sped out of there as fast as possible. On the way home, the security manager was still a little freaked out as he said, "Dude, how in the hell did you talk your way out of that? I was sure we were going to jail. You are Teflon!" I smiled and said I had learned a lot of lessons on how to talk to Afghan leaders over the last five years. "You have to let him know you are subservient to him and push a lot of flattery. Only then can you exert your influence," I said with a grin.

Women's Program

Even though irrigation was our main focus, we also wanted to ensure that women were not left out of the program. Since our program was focused on labor-intensive projects designed to get people working, it was a challenge to incorporate women into it. Women in Afghanistan, especially in the rural areas, were marginalized and expected to take care of the home. In order to get women involved in the program, we knew that we had to create a safe place where women could work on a project away from the eyes of men who may intimidate them or worse. We hired a local female program manager, whose entire job was focusing on the women's projects. The first thing she did was go to the director of Women's Affairs to discuss project ideas and get help finding needy women who could work on the projects. We decided to do a pilot project where women could work on a university building that desperately needed rehabilitation. The building was isolated behind walls so that no one would bother the women. The other big issue was training the women to do labor-intensive work, such as carpentry, painting, plastering, and roofing. Only men did those jobs, so we contacted the CTTC that my old Civil Affairs team had helped construct back in 2005 when I was in the Army. The training center helped by giving us a handful of skilled men who could teach and oversee the work done by the women.

We hired around 60 women and 6 men to complete the reconstruction of the university building in 50 days. The women were paid the same as the men, and each took home about $250 for the 50 days of work. The project was a success, and we then had a good idea to use for future women's projects. After the completion of the university building, we discovered that there were dozens of girls' schools in the city of Jalalabad that needed significant rehabilitation. We decided to create a project to fix all of the girls' schools in Jalalabad using female laborers, with a few male mentors. The program ended up being very successful. Altogether we spent $250,000 on the women's programs. We hired a total of 600 women and 50 male mentors. Together they rehabilitated a dozen school buildings in Jalalabad. That program was the only female labor program that anyone I know had heard of in Afghanistan, but perhaps there were others that I was not aware of.

Women Working on Rebuilding a Girls' School in Jalalabad

Kunar

Aside from our projects in the Nangarhar Province, our region also included the Kunar Province, which was far more dangerous. During a visit to the governor of Kunar in the first month of the job, driving down the road we became stuck in the middle of a firefight between a U.S. military convoy and a group of insurgents firing on them from the cliffs above the road. Wadi was driving the car that we were in and decided that it would be fun to drive right into the fighting, like a moron. I yelled at him to get off of the road, and he pulled into a small group of mud houses, where we took cover until the fighting stopped. One old man with a blown-off leg from stepping on a mine many years ago during the Soviet invasion saw me and invited our team to take shelter in his tiny house. He made us some tea, and we had a nice conversation while we listened to the bullets being fired near our vicinity. One of his neighbors actually yelled at him, "Why are you protecting the American!" The old man snapped back at him, loudly saying that it was his house, and I was his guest. I thought that was rather cool of him. Once the fighting stopped, we thanked the old man and were on our way back to Jalalabad.

Our Kunar projects followed the same basic principles as our Nangarhar projects and had similar success. The projects in Kunar rehabilitated thousands of acres of land in the districts of Khas Kunar and Asmar and helped reconstruct a village road in the Naray District. That was no small feat in an area that was highly unstable and tribally fragmented. One day we had a group of five men come to our gate, demanding to see me. They were village elders from the Asmar District, which was a good two- to three-hour drive from our compound. The men said that they had come just to thank us for the work that we had done in their villages. I was surprised that they would drive all that way just to give thanks.

Of course, the men asked for some more projects to be done, especially wells for drinking water. Stan happened to be visiting our site from Singapore and sat in on the meeting. At one point, in a joking manner Stan mentioned that they could throw the Taliban down the wells. The men suddenly got dead serious and said, "Who do you think is working on your projects?" They mentioned that many of the young men had joined the Taliban and other insurgency groups due to joblessness, but then they put down their weapons and picked up a shovel to work on our projects. They said that the men now have adequate water for their crops and are no longer going to be fighting. That was a huge deal to me and validated our program in the best way.

Workers Rebuilding an Intake Irrigation System in Kunar

Sources of Insurgency

All U.S. government agencies, including the military, liked to start talking about stopping the Taliban and other insurgency groups by focusing on stopping the "sources of insurgency." That phrase was constantly thrown around and became almost an annoyance. Nearly every briefing that I sat in mentioned that phrase. The idea was that we should work with the communities to find the root causes of people fighting, and then do projects or other initiatives that would help alleviate those causes. That all sounded logical and reasonable. The dilemma was that we were not really doing that. It would take years of trust-building and investigation to dig out all of those issues, and we certainly did not have time for trying to dissect all of the problems from thousands of villages in Afghanistan. Some smart people tried to build matrices and other systems to do that work with limited success, but there was often something missing afterward: ACTION!

It was easy to sit down and have conversations about the problems that Afghans faced, but if those conversations did not turn into significant actions to change the environment then they were a waste of time. Afghans constantly talked about how the U.S. government was not living up to the promises made by President Bush to rebuild Afghanistan, and they would be correct. Afghans wanted tangible results that would address the major issues that they had. In all of the polls that I read and briefings that I sat in on, there was one issue that was always ranked the No. 1 source of instability: unemployment. That was why I did not bother trying to flesh out every detail of every problem that Afghans had. We were going to address the big one by employing as many people as possible, and by doing so we would be doing the best thing that we could to counter the insurgency.

Accolades

I cannot even try to explain the pride that I had in our team. Those guys worked their butts off in extreme conditions, and did an amazing job overseeing thousands of workers and hundreds of projects with full transparency. Word got around pretty quickly, and everyone seemed to know whom we were and what we were doing. I showed up to a Nangarhar Provincial Council meeting that Governor Sherzai conducted each month. As soon as I walked in the door, Governor Sherzai asked for me to sit next to him at the head of the table. I think he was happy about how good we were making him look out in the districts. I was honored by the gesture even though I felt a little embarrassed by it. The USAID representative in the province quickly yelled out, "No!" very loudly. He said I should politely decline the gesture. I thought it would be very rude, but I quietly turned to the governor and said, "Sorry" through his interpreter. He kind of gave a disappointed look, but I think he understood that I was not being rude.

The Afghan government officials were not the only ones who took notice of our team's success. Johan, the man whom I respected most in the development world, and one of his colleagues called me to come over and talk about our projects. We had a great discussion about what each of us were doing on irrigation programs and made sure we were not overlapping and causing any conflicts in the districts. I pulled up our Google Earth map and showed him the hundreds of systems we had built in the last year. He was shocked and said, "Wow, you guys are doing great work, I better up my game." He may never know it, but that was probably the best compliment he could have given, since I looked up to him a lot.

CNN Visit

We were starting to wind down our projects for the year and prepare our plans for the next year when I got a call from the USAID representative in Kabul. He said that CNN Middle East Foreign Affairs Correspondent Jill Dougherty would be coming to Afghanistan and wanted to see some USAID projects. CNN had chosen our program to showcase on its exposé. I was excited that we were going to be able to show the world the work that we were doing. It was kind of comical, though, since Jill Dougherty had to ride around with a full military escort, and all kinds of protection and body armor, while I met her at our sites in a pickup truck wearing a polo shirt and khakis. I took her to some of the irrigation projects so that she could see the massive number of laborers that we were employing to rebuild the irrigation systems. I had some of the engineers brief her on what they were doing. They were beaming with pride as they explained how the systems worked and how they were fixing them. That impressed her, but what she was really interested in were the women's programs. She had heard that we were employing women doing labor projects, so she really wanted to see that for herself. We took her to one of our girls' schools, where the women were plastering and painting walls. I think she spent at least an hour talking to the women and taking pictures. I thought that she would have been more interested in the huge irrigation programs, but she only took 10 minutes to check those out. Later that year the program aired, and I was again bombarded by calls from friends who saw me on TV. It was great to get the team some much-deserved accolades.

The Year of the Chill

After all of the work that we had accomplished over the past year, we felt that we had the irrigation and school building stuff down to a science. Our region was adding the neighboring province of Laghman for the upcoming year, and I was already familiar with the place, so we were confident that we could replicate our success there, as well. We knew which districts we were going to focus on for the next year, so we made our plans early and were relaxed. We were calling it "the year of the chill," since we were so confident that it was going to be easy. The company brought all of the regional managers to Dubai to discuss the upcoming plans and how we would be expanding from 12 provinces to 19 provinces, and how there was going to be an enormous upgrade in the amount of money available for projects. Instead of a $50 million program, it was going to be more like a $125 million program, with $40 million designated specifically for the Kandahar Province. It was going to be one of USAID's largest community development programs in the world that year.

It was kind of crazy that a small company like ours was suddenly going to be running a massive program such as that. I guess that all of the work that we had done throughout the country was creating some excitement in Washington, D.C. I was happy to have done my part in our little corner of Afghanistan. Other provinces also had massive success and were as hungry as I was to get going on another great year. In order to pull off such a large undertaking, we were going to need to better organize ourselves and put more processes in place. Even though our work was good, we were still just a bunch of lightly organized, mostly ex-military guys who knew how to get things done but were not the best at following rules and procedures. That was going to have to change if we were going to ramp up to such a huge level and not screw up. I felt pain for Jim and the guys who were going to be running it, since it was going to be very stressful for them. But I was relaxed since our region was ready for the year of the chill.

Change of Plans

After I had arrived home on that long day in the field showing the CNN reporter around the projects, I received a Skype message from Stan. That was not all that uncommon, since Stan liked to keep his ear to the ground and would often write directly to regional managers and provincial managers, ignoring any chain of command. That would sometimes drive Jim nuts, since the big boss would sometimes find things out before he did, causing a bit of a rift. Stan asked how the CNN tour went, and I told him that it was great, and I thought the company would get some well-deserved praise for our work there. Stan wrote, "Great, then congratulations twice." I was almost afraid to ask, but I did anyway: "Why twice?" He said, "You are now the new senior program manager."

I guess Jim had decided that he had had enough of the program and was not getting along with Stan and the staff back in Singapore. I kind of fell back in my chair and actually said, "Fuck!" I was not really interested in doing it, since we already had our "year of the chill" planned out, and I was really looking forward to an easy year. I knew that suddenly running one of USAID's largest community development programs in the world was going to be a very big challenge. I was really comfortable in the city of Jalalabad and was so invested in the region that I did not want to leave and certainly not to live in frickin' Kandahar, where Jim had been running things from. I guessed that Stan knew that, since his next message was, "Don't worry, you can still stay in Jalalabad and run the program from there as the new headquarters." That eased my mind a bit, but building out seven new provincial staffs and their headquarters, as well as expanding the Kandahar operation due to a massive influx of funding, was going to be very tough. I was beginning to see why Jim had wanted to jump ship. As crazy as it was, it was an opportunity to really do something amazing, and I knew that I was up for the challenge, so I accepted. Stan simply replied, "Great, now get to Singapore, we have a lot to talk about."

Two days later I was on a long flight back to Singapore to meet with the company leadership team. I think that for some, meeting me was a bit of an eye-opener: a guy with no master's degree and one year of experience as a regional manager, and they were going to let me run that huge program. Normally people with 20 years of experience and fancy educations are chosen for that kind of role. I was pretty humbled by the whole thing. I laid out for the team the concept of comprehensive development that we had been doing in my old region, and how we could take the same concept and push it out to the other regions using the same processes and systems. There were some chuckles since there were really no procedures in place for anything except a simple finance process. I told them that I had written a procedure manual that I would farm out to the regions to simplify the process. That put some of the staff at ease. The different department heads all briefed me on everything from finance to internet systems, and I was ready to head back to Afghanistan and start the handover with Jim. It was going to be an interesting experience.

Handover

Going back to Afghanistan, I arrived in the city of Kandahar to spend two weeks with Jim and learn as much as I could from his experience as the senior program manager during the first two years of the program. At that point, Jim was pretty much fed up with the program and with CAC's leadership, and could not wait to get out. I did not know that there was so much bad blood between the Singapore headquarters team and Jim, but apparently it was pretty deep. Jim told me all about the problems that he had been having, especially with Singapore's finance team. The financial books were a mess, and that was one thing that could really get people into deep crap with the U.S. government. Jim told me how he organized his files, approved projects, oversaw finance and security, and generally kept the ship running.

Jim was not the only person leaving the program. Several members of his leadership team were leaving with him, which meant that I needed to build a whole new leadership team along with expanding the program by more than double. Jim and I looked at all of the personnel holes that needed to be filled, and he made some recommendations on who could step up and fill some of the key roles. Not being too familiar with the other regions, I counted on his knowledge to get me started on that. Jim would be leaving shortly, so I got as much info from him as I could, and then he kind of checked out for the last few days. The guys who were leaving spent most of their time partying up on the roof and generally not giving a damn, since their days were numbered.

The provincial manager of the Kandahar Province, Seth, was an interesting Scotsman, whom I had met earlier because he had come through Jalalabad for training before going down to Kandahar. He was a loud and pretty obnoxious guy, who had a giant beard that he spent nearly all of his time combing. Jim assured me that he was a great manager and that I should push to keep him around, but also that he had been considering leaving. I had a short meeting with him to feel out his intentions, hoping to retain as many experienced guys as I could. He told me that he was on the fence about staying and invited me to one of his morning meetings with his staff the next day. I was happy to sit in to get a feel for the work that they were doing. I also met his deputy provincial manager, a soft-spoken Nepalese guy named Bob.

The next morning, I arrived at the meeting in the large conference room. It was filled with at least 20 of the Kandahar office Afghan staff members, the south regional manager, Seth, and Bob. Seth introduced me as the incoming senior program manager and then began his meeting. I was expecting a cordial meeting, with Seth discussing each project and finding out any issues and recommending guidance. Instead, I saw the biggest bastardization of leadership I had ever witnessed. Seth would call out one staff member at a time and then lambast them for some perceived screw up. He was yelling at the top of his lungs, telling them to "Shut up" anytime they tried to explain the reasons why things were not going the way he had wanted. He would not let them speak at all. It was like a "Seinfeld" Festivus airing of grievances. The staff simply cowered and hung their heads. I looked at Seth, and he turned to me with a grin on his face like that was fun for him. The regional manager just sat quietly like it was business as usual. Bob sat there with his head lowered, like he was equally appalled but knew there was nothing he could do about it. Later in the day, Seth came to my room to tell me that he had decided to leave the program with Jim. I was relieved since it saved me the trouble of firing him. I remember telling my colleagues how I could not wait to get out of there, as that place was toxic. I suppose a couple years in that environment had weighed on the guys, and they were done. As soon as that group left Kandahar and the new group came in, things immediately turned around.

Building a New Team

I left for Jalalabad soon after the crazy meeting in Kandahar and needed to focus on filling the personnel holes that were coming. Since we were adding seven more provinces to the program and expanding the Kandahar office into four separate offices, it was going to be a daunting challenge. I immediately started promoting the deputy provincial managers into the provincial manager roles. That included promoting Bob in Kandahar to be one of the new provincial managers to replace Seth when he left. That turned out to be a great call since Bob ended up kicking butt there during the next year. I then had to shuffle some of the good provincial managers into regional manager roles where needed. I then took a look at the resumes that I had received from HR in Singapore and tried to recruit the best candidates that we could find who had experience in the provinces that we would send them to. Like many businesses, a lot of the recruits came from word of mouth from other managers who knew people who could perform well. Hiring people for a place like Afghanistan can be a tricky thing, since it was not your typical job that just anyone could do. We needed seasoned professionals who understood the dynamics and security implications of a place where bad decisions could have disastrous consequences. We ended up with seven regions, each covering two to three provinces.

The management was not the only concern, of course. We also needed to staff up a new headquarters that was vastly understaffed. We needed to build an independent monitoring division that was not yet present, so that we could prove to the U.S. government that we were doing the work that we were claiming to be doing. We also needed a new finance team since the last finance manager left with the Canadians in Kandahar. We also needed reporting staff, logistics, and other ancillary services that were either empty or neglected. And, we decided to create a headquarters office in Kabul, so that we could better coordinate with our donor, USAID, on a more regular basis. Since I was going to run the program from Jalalabad, it was good to have a place in Kabul to station all of our support systems for the country.

Our program had grown so large and had so many eyes on it that we also needed to put in place a chief of party role that had overall responsibility for the program. Although my position had taken on that role over the past two years, the program would require more clout. I received a call from Rani telling me that they wanted to put in place a chief of party to help me, since it was such a huge task. At the time, the reporting manager, Monica, had good experience, as well as a master's degree that I did not have at the time. Rani wanted to make sure that I was okay with it; it sounded like she was worried that I would feel betrayed that someone would be placed above me. I told her that it was all right and having help with the ancillary processes was great. I just wanted to run the program.

Monica and I got together and hashed out our responsibilities. Essentially she would reside in Kabul and have full control of non-project-related decisions, and I would handle all field decisions from Jalalabad. It would not have worked well if we had massive egos, but luckily we did not. Our relationship worked great. We talked nearly every day on the phone to ensure that we were on the same page; and when we did not agree we did not fight, we just worked out a compromise. I did not push her on non-field issues, and she let me make the calls on projects and people in the field. We had a solid trust in each other, and that was refreshing. I was focused and ready to start working on building the program. We only had one year to pull a rabbit out of the hat, and the clock had just started ticking.

Let's Do This

As soon as all regional managers were in place, I called a meeting of them and support managers at the office in Jalalabad. Since CAC had its own fleet of small planes, it was easy to just do a pick up of everyone and get them to Jalalabad in one day. Once everyone arrived, we got down to business and gathered together for a briefing. I wanted to introduce everyone to the new leadership team, explain everyone's roles, and let them know how we were going to operate that year. In prior years, there were very few rules and procedures. Everything from project proposals to project execution was kind of done on the fly, creating confusion and leading to conflict. I wanted to streamline the operation to work as smoothly as possible and avoid those problems. I gave each person a handbook that outlined every process needed to successfully run the offices and projects. I made the case that with so much funding and work expected of us over the next year that we would need to focus on large-impact projects as opposed to small projects. I outlined how we had worked in my region over the past year, building massive projects that contained dozens of sub-projects to have a greater impact. I showed them how we surged projects in particular districts in order to have a lasting effect. I mandated that irrigation be the main focus in rural areas and the reasons why.

Not everyone agreed with that approach. The guys working in the other provinces were mostly used to smaller projects that had less risk and were easier to manage. I told them, "That was fine for last year, but now you all have the experience and ability to step it up a notch and create real impact." Although I was a bit skeptical that my approach would work everywhere, it turned out that it did. I tasked the guys to get back to the regions and start working on the proposals. Within two weeks, the proposals started coming to me for approval. I was shocked at what I saw. Some of the proposals were huge projects — as high as a million dollars each — while some of them were a little less ambitious. Regardless, the team was on the right track, and our first wave of projects totaled about $15 million worth, slated for the first quarter of work. Not a bad start.

Visiting the Provinces

Each province in Afghanistan is unique, with its own set of challenges. Some are so high up in the Hindu Kush Mountains that it snows most of the year with only a narrow window to actually do projects. Some are relatively flat, with large, sandy desert areas. Some are a combination of mountains and river valleys fed from the snowmelt from the mountains. A few have large cities, like Nangarhar, Kandahar, and Herat. Others have no major urban areas, like Qalat and Logar. It was my goal to try to get to each of our 19 provinces to see the projects in person and help mentor the teams on the ground. That was not easy, since so much was going on around the provinces, and I was constantly bombarded with emails and calls to help solve issues. I certainly slept very little at night, and when I did I slept with my iPad next to me so that I could start reading emails before I even got out of bed. There was always a minimum of 50 emails in my inbox when I woke up.

There were three main sectors of infrastructure that we focused on across the country. Irrigation system rehabilitation consisted of about 70 percent of projects. Another 20 percent focused on municipal infrastructure in the cities where we would rehabilitate sidewalks, drainage systems, and roads. About 5 percent focused on school and clinic rehabilitation, and another 5 percent was dedicated to other projects. The teams in the provinces mostly adhered to the comprehensive model that I had shared with them. Instead of fixing small things, they tackled big issues. Enormous 20-mile irrigation canals were dug, dams were built, impassable mountain roads were opened up to cars for the first time, the road and sidewalk networks of entire towns were fixed, flood protection was built for towns, and even an airport runway was constructed.

Having our own planes allowed me the ability to access some of the most remote provinces. Often I would be the only passenger. Very few flights went to some of the provinces that we worked in and for good reason. It was dangerous to land on some of the dirt runways, and the planes were even shot at from the ground from time to time. We employed several South African bush pilots who seemed to fly with nerves of steel. Once after we had landed at one remote airstrip, the pilot got out to check the plane, only to see an AK-47 round had been shot into the lower fuselage. That was a little nerve-racking. When I was flying as a lone passenger the pilots would have a little fun by flying low along the earth or diving straight down into an airstrip, or doing corkscrew maneuvers. At one point after a crazy landing, the pilot got out and started smoking next to the plane. I said, "Geez, that was a heck of a landing, I thought we were going to hit the side of the mountain!" He just grinned and took a puff of smoke. In a thick South African accent he said, "Don't worry bru. Ya gotta remember, we aren't trying to die either, trust me." Those guys were so good at flying those small twin-engine planes that it was like flying with stunt pilots.

Nimroz

One of the first provinces that I wanted to visit was the most remote province of Nimroz. The main town of Zaranj sat right on the border with Iran. The airport was used almost exclusively for our planes, since we were one of the only companies flying in there. The airport manager would have the gravel runway graded right before we arrived just to make sure that we would land safely. We were doing a number of irrigation projects there, some of which skirted the Iranian border. As I walked down the irrigation canals I could see the Iranian border guards in the watchtowers looking down at me. I waved, but all I got back were snarly looks. I thought that was kind of rude (just kidding). The provincial manager there was a well-educated Afghan guy named Bahar. He was very intelligent and knew the place well. He might have been the most popular man in Nimroz for all of the amazing work that he did. As soon as he met me at the plane he walked me to our house/office nearby and then took me straight to meet the provincial governor.

The Governor invited me to his office and told me how much he appreciated all of the work being done for his province and how happy he was with Bahar. Then they took me on a tour of the projects. Bahar was working on some of the most impressive development projects in the country. His team focused mainly on large irrigation projects, and rehabilitating roads and drainage ditches in the cities. The irrigation projects constructed over 400 miles of irrigation canals that turned over 25,000 acres of desert into usable farmland. It was an amazing feat. He also constructed a large dam that diverted wastewater into a reservoir that fed another large canal system. He hired over 18,000 people to build much of the canal by hand, creating major employment for the year. Those were game-changing projects for the province that would have a lasting impact well after we were gone.

A Completed Intake System in Nimroz

Kandahar

After seeing the great successes that Bahar was having in Nimroz, I wanted to see the work being done in our main focus province of Kandahar. Most of the work there was happening in the populated areas around the city of Kandahar and its suburbs. Kandahar is an ancient city, founded by Alexander the Great over 2,000 years ago, as one of the many Alexandrias that he had created throughout his empire, including several in Afghanistan. Once a thriving commercial center, that old city had seen better days, and three decades of war and neglect had left the city's infrastructure in a state of disrepair.

The team there was focused on a few main areas. First, they wanted to get the city healthier by allowing the sewage draining systems and flood spillways to function properly to flush out waste, especially human waste, to combat disease. The team rebuilt miles of drainage canals and spillways to allow the system to finally start flushing away sewage. That was a Herculean task that needed a small army of workers to complete. Ours were just the guys to do it.

A Completed Drainage System in Kandahar

Bob and his team took me on a tour of their projects, and the first place was the assembly plant that they built to construct concrete covers for the roadside ditches that collected human waste and other nasty stuff from the roads. They needed to create thousands of those covers to span miles of the rebuilt concrete ditches they had constructed. The assembly line was made up of hundreds of Afghan men cutting steel rebar, assembling the parts, pouring concrete molds, and then transporting the finished concrete blocks by crane truck to the work sites. It looked like an army of ants moving in unison, each knowing where they were going and what they were doing. It was so well organized that they were able to create hundreds of blocks each week. I was so impressed that Bob had taken a team that only weeks before had been on the verge of anarchy and transformed it into a model of efficiency. It shows what good leadership and vision can achieve, and the guys in Kandahar had certainly brought their A game.

Bob's team was only one of four teams that we created for the Kandahar metro area. Other teams focused on the suburbs of the city of Kandahar in the areas of Arghandab, Panjwai and Daman. The Arghandab team focused on projects similar to the ones that Bob was doing, since Arghandab was more urban, but the Panjwai and Daman teams focused mainly on large-scale irrigation projects, such as mile-long karez systems and canals off of the rivers. Those areas were much more dangerous than the city center, so projects were more challenging to complete.

The Panjwai leader, John, took me out to visit his irrigation projects, and as we drove to the sites we passed up field after field of marijuana plants. That was a change from the opium poppy fields that I was used to in other areas. Men were out working in the fields without a care in the world about law enforcement. No one dared to interfere with those illegal cash crops. The scenery driving to Panjwai was breathtaking. The jagged sandstone mountains that separated Panjwai from the city of Kandahar shot straight out of the ground in an otherwise flat area, like they did not belong. It would be a beautiful recreation spot if not for the security concerns. John took me to eat lunch at the local U.S. Army outpost nearby. We had a lunch out of a box and sat on some wooden stools and chatted with some of the commanders of the nearby units. They were all surprised that we were able to conduct work in such a dangerous place, while driving around in cruddy Toyota Corollas and blending in. That was not what they were used to. Although the projects in Panjwai were not as large scale as other areas, it was clear that John was doing his best in a challenging place.

The Daman leader, Troy, also took me out to see his large irrigation projects in Daman and meet the district governor there. Troy was an ex-Army guy, whom I had to talk into taking the job. I knew that he was a tough guy who could handle the stress of the place and was able to work well with the Afghans. He did not disappoint. The karez rehabilitation projects that he worked on reminded me a lot of the karez systems we worked on in Nangarhar when I was the regional manager there the prior year. Those systems were hundreds of years old, if not a thousand. From the air, you could see the manholes that served the underground canals that ran for miles. They looked like a bombing run had been done from an old World War II attack. Troy's team was stabilizing each manhole and ensuring that the karez would continue feeding water to farm fields for the next millennium.

The Kandahar teams overall managed to complete 50 large projects that year. About half of the projects were focused on city infrastructure, a quarter on irrigation, and another quarter on road rehabilitation. They ended up hiring over 32,000 people in the city of Kandahar and the surrounding suburbs. They reconstructed nearly 125 miles of irrigation and drainage canal systems, rebuilt nearly 62 miles of roads, and constructed over 80 miles of sidewalks in the city of Kandahar. That was, by far, the most aggressive province, where nearly a quarter of our money was spent.

Before leaving Kandahar, I had a meeting with the deputy governor, who was an American resident who had fled Afghanistan years before and had returned to serve his country. He was delighted with the work that we were doing in the province and showed his gratitude to our company and USAID. He seemed like a genuine guy and warned of how dangerous Kandahar could be. That must have been an omen since insurgents killed him not long after our meeting. Although I did not know him well, I had a soft spot for those who left a comfortable, safe life in the U.S. to come back and try to help their country, only to be gunned down for their efforts.

Uruzgan

While I was already down south, I took a quick flight up to our office in the province of Uruzgan. That province was very isolated in the south-central part of the country and was known as a very dangerous and unstable place. The provincial manager, Leo, and the regional manager for the south, Christian, picked me up and took me on the short drive into the capital, Tarinkot. The town was a dry and dusty place that would make anyone depressed just driving through it. The office was a pretty rundown old building, but the staff was happy and motivated.

The managers and I talked about the projects and any issues they were facing and gave me a good briefing on the province. We built a campfire and had a few beers that night, discussing the way forward for the area. Leo was a positive guy, who I really liked a lot. It was easy to tell that he enjoyed the work that he did and took pride in helping to rebuild Afghanistan. There was no one better suited to that environment and getting things done in such a challenging province. His projects focused almost exclusively on rebuilding the roads, walkways, and sewage drainage systems in the Tarinkot and the more remote city of Dehrawud. By the time they were done, nearly every neighborhood in the cities was touched by their work.

The only other project they completed was a 16-mile road project called the

Chuta Road, which linked an isolated area of the province to the main commercial center. Much of the road ran alongside a river that had eroded away the road, cutting the area off from trade and security services. The area was overrun by insurgents due to its isolation, and it was vital that the roadway be restored. The team constructed protection walls and rebuilt the road, restoring those services. It was a major accomplishment in an area that was extremely dangerous to work in. Overall, the Uruzgan team hired over 11,000 people throughout the year on their projects, which was an amazing feat in that area.

The team took me down to visit the governor of the province and have dinner at his home. He was very happy to have us visit and treated us like royalty. As we sat down on the floor to have dinner, the power went out in the compound, and it was a bit freaky. It did not help that the sound of gunfire in the distance kept echoing through the evening. We ended up dining by flashlight that night, while listening to stories of the guys who fought the Soviets in the 1980s and the Taliban more recently. As nice as the dinner was, I was happy when we left and got back to the office for the night.

On a separate trip later in the year, I was invited to fly up by helicopter to the northern district of Gizab in Uruzgan. That district was effectively cut off from the rest of the province — and pretty much the entire country. It was a beautiful mountainous district that looked like it was 300 years behind the modern world. There was no modern infrastructure, and the people there had not seen many foreigners since the Russian invasion. CAC had a separate program in Gizab to help the community, working with a U.S. Special Forces team based there. We landed and walked through the area. As we walked down the only main street in a small village the people stared at us from the small shops in the market. They looked at us like aliens had just landed. It was pretty uncomfortable, but I was used to it by then. The team started working on roads and irrigation projects in the area shortly after our visit, and some of the guys told me that there were posters put up all over the market with my picture on them. I guess someone took a picture, and I became a local celebrity even though I was not actually part of that program. I got a good laugh out of that. Unfortunately, the U.S. military contracting officer for that program screwed up and canceled the project for some unknown reason. Cutting off funding in the middle of the project upset the local population in a big way. The contractor's stupidity put our staff's lives in danger and put the U.S. Special Forces team in a difficult position, as well, not to mention caused one big fiasco.

Later in the year, Leo and Christian were both fired for improper accounting on the projects. They certainly were not stealing money, but they played with the procurement rules in order to make projects run without getting permission for changes. It was complicated, but even though they did not do the right thing I was not happy to see them go after all of the amazing work they had done, and I felt they deserved a second chance. I was overruled on that decision and had to let them go. There were some parts of the job that sucked, but it is part of leadership.

Helmand

As I continued visiting our provinces in the south, my next stop was Helmand. I had a particular distaste for that place after spending six months there with the counternarcotics team a few years before. The CAC team actually occupied a decades-old compound there that had been the headquarters of the old USAID project in the 1960s to build out the dam and irrigation infrastructure that still makes the deserts of Helmand bloom today. However, much of that infrastructure was in a bad state of decay and needed reconstruction. The provincial manager, Henry, and the regional manager, Tom, who I had installed there as a favor a year after he got me the initial job with CAC in Nangarhar, were in charge of the program there. The two of them butted heads regularly, and there was clearly a lack of cohesion with the Afghan staff.

Tom also caused me headaches with the USAID leadership. As much as I loved Tom, he was a roughneck ex-Marine who liked to carry his pistol on his hip like John Wayne. Everyone else kept weapons hidden and used their security, so that we "aid workers" did not appear to be mercenaries or threats to anyone. USAID alerted me at least twice that Tom should not be openly carrying his weapon, but Tom loved to chant about his Second Amendment rights and how important carrying his weapon was.

Helmand was a mess as a province. The infrastructure was crumbling everywhere. Most of the province was very insecure and unsafe to travel in. The government was inept and corrupt. That all led it to be a very challenging place to help run a successful program in at the scale I would liked to have seen. Regardless of the challenges, the team there did some successful work. Most of the work in Helmand consisted of rebuilding urban roads, constructing sewage and drainage ditches, and rebuilding commercial areas in major towns to allow for commerce and trade to take hold again. The team also managed to work in a few women's projects, such as sewing curtains, pillows, and uniforms for schools and government buildings. In all, the team employed about 9,000 people that year and did the best it could in one of the toughest places.

One of the biggest disappointments I had with Helmand was the lack of vision that the USAID representative had there. I was waiting for Henry outside of a tent on the military base where all U.S. government officials had their offices. Henry was in a meeting at the time, and I struck up a conversation with a woman who happened to be one of the USAID representatives in Helmand. I asked her if she was aware of our program there, and she said, "Yeah, that is 'cash for work' stuff that really doesn't interest me. We are looking at doing bigger projects other than the small stuff you guys do." I was surprised at how ignorant she was of our work, so I calmly asked her, "What are some of the major issues you are looking to solve?" She told me that they had hundreds of water gate systems that controlled the water in the hundreds of miles of canals that feed the farmland. So many were damaged and decayed and needed fixing, along with shoring up the canals themselves. I told her about the many huge canal rehabilitation programs that we were doing all over the country and how we could have put together a comprehensive program to fix a lot of those problems if she just sat down and talked to our managers. She was surprised to hear that and said she would look into it. Of course, nothing came of it. What a missed opportunity to do some great work in a much-needed place!

Zabul

The last stop on the southern tour was Zabul. That province was a dusty, dry area that had been hit by droughts and the insurgency and was a very dangerous place. More than half of the population counted on farming and animal husbandry to make ends meet, but with the harsh conditions the vast majority of the population suffered from food insecurity. We wanted to focus our efforts on rural irrigation to help the farmers get back on their feet, but we were often unable to get security guarantees from the population, something that was rare for our program. We instead focused nearly all attention on the major population centers, where much of the population had migrated to due to the droughts and security issues.

Despite the security concerns, the team was able to work with the government to rehabilitate roads, sidewalks, and drainage systems in the major towns of Qalat and Shahjoy. The team was able to employ nearly 12,000 people to rebuild 5 miles of roads, 35 miles of sidewalks, 11 miles of drainage ditches, and a large karez irrigation system. The huge influx of $4 million of wages paid to the population was a big boost to a province with only 350,000 people. In the end, nearly 20 percent of the families in Zabul benefited directly from working on the projects. The projects also benefited the urban populations by spurring economic growth and enhancing health conditions with improved sanitation. Zabul was a tough assignment for the team there. I was very proud of the work that the group was able to accomplish in such harsh conditions.

Workers Building a Sidewalk and Drainage Ditch in Zabul

Nangarhar

After a couple of weeks in the southern provinces, I finally got back home to Jalalabad in the Nangarhar Province. Since turning over the reins of the eastern region to the new team, I wanted to get caught up on their projects and visit some of the field sites. The Nangarhar team basically continued to expand on the comprehensive irrigation rebuilding program and the women's program that we had started to rebuild schools. Aside from floods that hampered several of the projects that year, things went pretty smoothly in Nangarhar. The leadership was excellent, and the engineers did a great job keeping up with the crazy amount of work assigned to them.

The team was able to accomplish a remarkable amount of work in a short period of time. Altogether, the team rebuilt over 200 irrigation systems in the rural districts and 10 schools in the city of Jalalabad. Around 20,000 people were hired to do the work. At the end of the program, our company had rebuilt about 20 percent of the small irrigation systems in Nangarhar in just two years. Imagine what we could have done if given five years! Between our program and some of our sister programs, the vast majority of irrigation systems in the central part of the Nangarhar Province were rehabilitated to some degree. Several of the outer districts, unfortunately, did not get the same attention. I would have loved to see them all rebuilt, which I feel would have helped stabilize those dangerous areas, but we could only do so much with the time and budget that we had.

Kunar

The Kunar projects followed up on the prior year's work by rebuilding several large canal systems in the Khas Kunar District. The two 10-mile-long canals that fed nearly all arable land in that district were falling apart, and at least 30 percent of the land in that district was not farmable. The team executed an ambitious plan to rebuild the systems, hiring over 8,000 people throughout the year to do it. I looked at before and after satellite photos of the area. The amount of greenery in the after pictures proved that those canal rebuilding projects drastically changed the landscape, allowing for cultivation of virtually any crop, and lands that were once abandoned were producing excellent crops.

Masons Finishing a Canal Wall in Kunar

The team also managed to rebuild several irrigation systems in the remote district of Asmar, which was a very dangerous place to go. The team worked out a partnership with the local villagers and was able to rebuild several smaller systems. In the end, nearly all of the irrigation systems in the Asmar District were rebuilt. The team then got a little too ambitious, though. The district of Nurgal was the next target district, and the team tried to rebuild the two major canal systems there. One of the systems went well, but the other system was a fiasco. We had a pretty strict rule that we would only rebuild existing systems and would not try to change the way the water flowed. That helped us to avoid mistakes that could harm the system or hurt the way farmers would get their water. In Nurgal, the team told me that the villagers wanted to try to expand the system and thought that they could add more land by doing it. I was very reluctant and sent the engineers to check on the feasibility of doing that. The engineers said it was doable, so I relented and signed off on the project. Unfortunately, the engineers were wrong, and to make a long story short the project ran into serious problems and was not completed. It was a tough lesson learned. However, in the end the team did a lot of awesome work, hiring over 12,000 people that year and transforming the irrigation infrastructure of three major districts.

Laghman

The small province of Laghman was another irrigation success story in the eastern region. Laghman only had five districts, and 70 percent or more of the population lived in the districts of Qarghayi and Mihtarlam. We focused our efforts in those two districts. The irrigation systems in there consisted of large canal systems that fed off of the two major rivers running through the province. The team put together an amazing plan to rebuild all of the major systems in one year. The projects were a huge success. In that amount of time, the team rebuilt over 18 miles of canals, hiring over 7,000 people. The province had a major increase in farmable land, and the local government was shocked at the efficiency of the work. When I had met with the provincial governor originally, he did not believe such an amount of work was feasible in a year. At the end of the year, he was very grateful for the work and economic boost that the projects gave to his province. The only regret I had was that we only were allowed to work in Laghman for one year. If we had one more year to operate there, we would have been able to rebuild the entire irrigation infrastructure of the province. That would have been incredible.

Wardak

After spending a couple of weeks at home in Nangarhar, it was time to hit the road again and get to some of the other provinces. I took some time to check in at our headquarters in Kabul and meet with the USAID representative there. After that I was able to take a short drive to the Wardak Province to check on the large projects happening there. The team in Wardak had completed several small projects the year before, and now was joining the rest of the country in doing massive irrigation and municipal infrastructure projects. The provincial capital of Maidan Shar received a huge project to rebuild all streets, sidewalks, and drainage ditches in the town. It was a huge project, employing over 2,500 people. When it was complete, it looked like a whole new city. The mayor of the town was delighted with the work that transformed his small city in a matter of months. The other projects focused on five large irrigation canal systems. Altogether, the team rebuilt over 88 miles of irrigation canals, constructed 20 miles of floodwalls for several villages, and hired over 6,000 people to do the work. It was a huge success.

Logar

I then took a short drive to the nearby Logar Province, where the provincial manager, Troy, was a former military guy, as well. He kept his program very simple. The team focused on rebuilding the four main irrigation canal systems in the province. In total, the team hired around 4,000 people to rebuild 40 miles of canal systems and 6 miles of floodwalls for the villages. I had not spent much time in Logar that year, but at the end of the year I went down to the province for the weekend to help close down the program there. Troy, and I finally got a chance to sit down and reflect on the year, and to get to know each other.

We were very different people, but both being ex-military gave us a brothers-in-arms kinship. By the end of the night, we had finished a bottle of vodka, laughed hysterically, and enjoyed chatting about the program. After polishing off the bottle, we were pretty drunk when Troy turned to me and slurred, "Hey, dude, you mind if I burn some hash?" I laughed because the odor of marijuana was already very obvious there, and even though that was not my kind of thing I figured what the heck. Guys have to do whatever gets them through the job there, I guess. I said, "Go ahead, it's not for me, but I'm not going to object." Troy brought out a good-sized bag of pot and proceeded to roll several blunts with it. We had a fun night hanging out. A few years after the program had ended I met a lady who had been the USAID representative in Logar. She knew our program well and said that in all of her time in Logar our program was the best one she had ever seen. I thought that was the highest compliment we ever got and gave me a good sense of peace for what we had achieved there.

Workers Rebuilding a Canal System in Logar

Ghazni

Ghazni was well known as a dangerous place and very tough to work in. It took a substantial effort from our team there to accomplish anything. The Ghazni team decided to focus solely on irrigation projects, since that was most needed and the one area where nobody would disagree. Several of the villages had old rivalries and animosity toward each other. The large-scale irrigation canal and karez projects that the team undertook helped to bring many of those villages together during implementation and got them to sit down and hash out their differences. The team focused nearly all of its attention around the northern part of the province since it was the only accessible area. The team rebuilt over 35 miles of irrigation canals and karez systems, and constructed over 28 miles of floodwalls, while hiring nearly 7,000 people. It was a major win in such a challenging place. Despite the successes, two of the major projects had to be canceled prior to completion due to the security situation. That was rare for our projects, and only happened if the area became too dangerous and the village leaders could not guarantee security.

Paktia

The team in Paktia ran its projects a bit differently. Instead of large-scale irrigation or municipal projects, the team there decided to do a broader spectrum of small projects. It did focus a lot on irrigation projects, but also focused on school and government building rehabilitation, greenhouse projects, and even a micro-hydro electric project. Paktia was one of the most dangerous places to work, so I left the project decisions up to the team and supported whatever it felt was best. At the end of the year, team members started seeing the light on the larger scale irrigation projects and did a couple of those, as well. The project sites in Paktia were so remote and away from the main population centers, so the team needed very close coordination and buy-in from the local village leaders. It received that support mainly due to our connections with one of the tribal chiefs of the area. Ajmal, the tribal chief, was a good friend of our company's owner and wanted to see a lot of help given to the region that he represented. Ajmal clearly had his detractors, as well. During a visit from Ajmal, his vehicles came under attack, and our team was caught in the middle of it. Luckily there were no casualties, but it did shake up the team a bit. Nevertheless, our team drove on and was able to accomplish great projects in areas no other aid agency would dare go to. The team ended up hiring over 10,000 people that year, reconstructing over 15 miles of canals, rebuilding 45 miles of floodwalls, and 3 miles of roads, among other projects.

Paktika

Paktika is a neighboring province to Paktia and had many of the same security issues. The team there focused mostly on irrigation projects, a few municipal buildings, a hospital rehabilitation, and a roadway reconstruction. Paktika was also a large province with villages spread out all over without very good road access. The team had to rely a lot on its government partnerships to get anything accomplished. Despite the challenges, the team did quite well, hiring over 6,000 people to rehabilitate over 20 miles of canals, reconstruct 2 miles of roadway, and construct 10 miles of floodwalls. The team also was able to reconstruct a major health clinic that was in desperate need of repair. The prior health clinic was literally falling apart and was itself a health hazard. When I got a chance to visit the new structure, it was a clean facility that was pretty much rebuilt from the ground up. Although that was not typical of our work, I was proud that the guys took on the challenge and were able to complete it.

Khost

Like Paktia and Paktika, Khost was a very dangerous area, with a significant security problem due to its location on the Pakistan border. It was a well-known hub for terrorist infiltration, and there was a lot of local support for the bad guys out in the rural areas. Despite the security concerns, the Khost team ran one of the most efficient programs in the country. The team focused mainly on irrigation and floodwall construction and worked at a pace unmatched in the country. The team was able to spread its projects out through almost the entire province, with strong cooperation from the government and local leaders. Visiting the province, I was struck by the efficiency and excellent planning that the teams did to make their projects run on time and on budget. None of their projects were canceled despite working in some of the most dangerous places in Afghanistan. The team hired over 14,000 people, rebuilt 15 miles of irrigation canals and 8 miles of roads, and constructed a mind-boggling 52 miles of floodwalls that saved dozens of villages from destruction during annual floods. The team was able to accomplish all of that while living in an area that was difficult to move around in and was cut off from much of the country.

Workers Rebuilding a Canal System in Khost

Herat

After taking a break from visiting the eastern provinces, later in the year I traveled to see the work being done in the western provinces. Herat is the main city and province in western Afghanistan. It borders Iran and Turkmenistan, and was known for being a much safer area than the volatile eastern provinces, although it still had its problem districts. The Herat team focused most of its attention on the more insecure districts of Shindand and Injil. USAID felt that other aid agencies were able to handle the more secure areas of the province, so they asked us to work in the tougher districts. The team spent most of its time on irrigation and road reconstruction. The province had one of the smallest project portfolios, since much more attention was given to the eastern provinces. In total, the team hired nearly 3,000 people, rebuilt 31 miles of irrigation and drainage canals, rehabilitated nearly 25 miles of roadways, and built 3 miles of floodwalls. Although the living conditions in the city of Herat were pretty safe and comfortable compared to other provinces, the team did its work in the most dangerous areas, making it a tough challenge.

Farah

Another one of the western provinces bordering Iran, Farah was a volatile place where it was difficult to work, however, that did not stop the amazing team there that managed to employ over 23,000 people to work on mostly irrigation and road rehabilitation. Only our Kandahar offices hired more people that year. The Farah team took the idea of surging large projects into districts and put it into overdrive. The team was able to accomplish huge projects in a short period of time. Besides irrigation and roads, the team also did some great community projects, such as building a large park and rehabilitating a women's education center using women workers. Altogether, the team rebuilt 87 miles of road, 250 miles of irrigation and drainage canals, rehabilitated 12 buildings, and built 12 miles of floodwalls. To this day, I do not know how they pulled that off, but I could not be prouder of the team there.

Badghis

The Badghis team had one of the shortest time frames to accomplish its projects. The province, situated on the Turkmenistan border, was very remote, and it took a long time to get the office set up and staff situated. The team only had less than 10 months to accomplish the work but made the most of it. The team focused on irrigation, completing major repairs to three main systems that fed much of the irrigated land in northern Badghis. The team rebuilt over 87 miles of irrigation canal systems and constructed 5 miles of floodwalls. The team hired over 7,500 people to do the work in the most dangerous pockets of Badghis. In such a short period of time, the team was able to accomplish an amazing amount of work.

Daikundi

One of the few provinces that I was not able to visit was the remote central mountain province of Daikundi. That place was only accessible by U.N. helicopter, and our guys would often get stranded there for weeks waiting on a flight, so I did not take the risk of going. It was a beautiful place and relatively safe. The province was under snow much of the year due to its high elevation. Our team there managed only a few projects in the short time that we had worked there over the year. The team managed to build sidewalks through the main city center and constructed a road to the cut-off southern districts, but the main focus for the team was building an airport so that the province could access the rest of the country. Although that was unlike anything that we had ever done, I figured what the hell. The old airstrip was unusable and consisted of a dirt strip on top of a mountain that was too short to land any decently sized plane. The team got to work extending the airstrip by filling and building out the mountaintop as much as possible. The middle of the airstrip also had a giant granite bolder sticking out of it. Since we could not excavate it, we got some local support from the community that came in with explosives and blew it up. Bombs were never in short supply in Afghanistan! After excavating and filling the airstrip, the team was able to level it, and small planes were able to fly in and out for the first time. The team hired over 2,500 people to do the work, and the provincial governor was very happy to have a way to join Daikundi to the rest of Afghanistan.

Aircraft Landing at the New Airport in Daikundi

Ghor

The only other province that I was not able to get to was Ghor. Situated in the central part of the country, like Daikundi, it was not very easy to get to. The province was sparsely populated, and flights rarely went there. I did fly into the airport once on a stopover but was not able to visit the office. The place was so dry and desolate that it looked like a landscape straight out of "Star Wars." Since Ghor was so remote and cut off from the country, the team there focused entirely on road rehabilitation. The guys hired around 4,000 people to reconstruct the roads and hired hundreds of women to build gabion wire structures for protection walls to stop floods from damaging the roads. The roads they built were able to connect much of the province to other hubs in the region, greatly helping trade and market access for farmers. In total, the team rebuilt 105 miles of roads and 2 miles of retaining walls.

Success!

By the end of the year when the smoke had cleared from all of that work, we had spent nearly $80 million on projects. We had hired over 200,000 people in short-term labor to build the projects. We had rebuilt over 1,200 miles of irrigation canal systems, enough to build a canal from Philadelphia to Miami! We had rebuilt over 370 miles of roads and constructed 310 cubic miles of floodwalls, protecting hundreds of small villages. We had also rebuilt over 50 schools and clinics, three parks, a stadium, and an airport. I think that we could definitely look back on the year and call it a huge success. After the year died down, USAID cut our program to only a handful of provinces in which the teams continued to do great work for another year. We certainly had hoped that USAID would continue to fund such a successful program for more years, but that funding would be later utilized to start up a new program that unfortunately would be far less successful. It was difficult to try to understand how our government makes those decisions, but it was not surprising based on some of the strange decisions made during my time in Afghanistan.

The most important ingredient to the success of the program was the Afghan local employees. There were approximately 1,500 Afghans employed by the company during the program. Those men and women worked harder than anyone I have ever seen to ensure that the program was successful. They risked their lives everyday going out into dangerous areas of the country, where Taliban and Al Qaeda insurgents were everywhere. The Afghan staff members were motivated to make a difference in their country and took a lot of pride in what they did. I do not think I could ever say enough about the job that they did and how proud I was to work with them each day.

End-of-the-Year Briefing

At the end of the year, I got a call from our USAID representative in Kabul, who asked me to give a briefing to one of the senior managers from USAID who came in from Washington, D.C. Apparently he had heard about our success and wanted to understand how we were doing business so that he could use it as a model for future programs. I laid out our entire approach to doing work and showed him how our direct route of working with communities with no subcontractors and no wasted money on huge security firms made our program so efficient. I used Laghman as an example and told him how we had rebuilt at least 70 percent of its irrigation systems in one year, and that if they funded us for just one more year we would have been able to finish it all. He turned to the representative in Kabul and asked why they had stopped funding that province. The guys struggled to tell him that they were going to be funding other programs and had to take the money from somewhere, so they took it from our program. The USAID executive then asked me if I would come to Washington, D.C., and brief the Afghanistan/Pakistan office on how we did our projects so that they could learn from it. Of course, I agreed. The next month I flew to D.C. and gave a briefing to a room full of young USAID staff members, who looked like they were fresh out of college. They were glued to the briefing, but I do not think it helped much. None of those guys were decision makers, so it was not like they were going to make any changes. I would like to hope that they would think about that briefing sometime when they are in a position to affect change, but I am not holding my breath.

Dealing with More Corruption and Theft

Although most projects went smoothly with very few reported corruption issues, there were plenty of shenanigans to deal with throughout that year. We had one straight-up theft in Kandahar, a strange embezzlement in Nangarhar, and unproven allegations of minor corruption in a few other provinces. Although allegations were made, it was difficult to ascertain proof in a place like Afghanistan, where corruption was rampant, and people did not like to talk for fear of retaliation. It was also common for people to unjustly accuse others of corruption, only to create problems for someone they disliked. Each of those issues showed the importance of processes and procedures when running a massive program.

The Kandahar theft was a failure of both leadership and not following procedures. The finance officer in Kandahar was in charge of a safe that contained millions of dollars in it. The safe was supposed to be locked at all times unless money distribution was taking place. The finance officer instead left the safe wide open and had left the room. One of the local Afghan staff members grabbed about $200,000 and left with it. Every night the provincial manager and finance officer conducted a cash count of the safe's money to ensure that it matched up with the account ledger. However, the provincial manager and finance officer skipped that step for a couple of days and just doctored their cash count sheets. The money was missing for days before anyone knew about it. Thankfully, the thieves were no masterminds.

CAC had hired a new country finance officer, Mark, who had a history of investigating fraud, and he was really good at it. A group of us flew down to the Kandahar office to find out what was going on. One of the local staff members did not show up for work for a couple of days since the theft, but his cousin, who also worked for us, did. Mark questioned him, and the guilt pretty much showed on his face. Although he claimed that he had no knowledge of the theft, we worked with one of the local police chiefs to throw him in jail for the night to enhance his memory. Although I do not know what happens in Afghan jails, I cannot believe that it was a great experience. The next day we went to the police station to question him again. He looked like a broken man. Mark went to work on him like a detective from a TV show. Mark said in a very loud tone, "Look, I know what happened, so you can stop pretending you don't know. Don't try to lie to me, because I am going to tell you right now I'm smarter than you, and you are going to tell me what I need to know." At first the young guy tried to play innocent with a quiet denial, but after being badgered by Mark for only a few minutes he fessed up. He said his cousin took the money and fled to the Ghazni District. The thief paid him about $20,000 for his help and to keep his mouth shut.

That guy was promptly fired, and money recovered, but we still had to locate the alleged perpetrator. We got in touch with the police in Ghazni and tracked down the thief at his family's house in Ghazni. He was arrested, and the money was recovered. Apparently, he had planned on fleeing to Pakistan with the money, but we got to him first. The two guys' families came to our compound screaming and protesting that their children were innocent, but both had confessed and became embarrassments to their families' honor. I do not really know what happened to those guys after that, but I was happy that we were able to recover the money.

The Nangarhar theft was even dumber. The Nangarhar office had contracted with a local supplier for concrete on one of our large irrigation projects. The logistics officer was tasked with going to the cement dealer's office and paying for the cement so that it could be delivered. That was a normal thing since we used thousands of bags of cement on each project. The logistics officer went to the cement dealer with around $100,000 in cash and came back with the receipt. Weeks later when our projects were running out of cement, we called the cement dealer to find out why we had not received our deliveries to the sites. The dealer said he had not been paid yet, even though we had the receipt of payment. The logistics officer had simply created a fake receipt and pocketed the money. After a thorough grilling by our security staff, the logistics officer admitted his theft and the money was recovered. I am not sure how that guy thought he could get away with that, but at least it ended well.

Despite those thefts and allegations of corruption, I was quite confident that our program was the most transparent program I had seen in Afghanistan. There were few programs that would be happy to open their account books for anyone to see at any time to prove where every dollar was spent. That was the promise I made to anyone who levied a complaint. I was proud to show that the vast majority of dollars spent in our program went to labor and materials on projects instead of to security firms and subcontractors. It was exceedingly more difficult to run a program that way, but in my opinion it was the best way to spend taxpayer money.

The way I approached spending money was to look at each project in terms of how many U.S. taxpayers paid for each project. The average federal tax bill for a typical family was $8,000. A typical large irrigation project for us cost about $160,000, so you could say that 20 average U.S. taxpayers paid for that project. Thinking about it that way helped me to personalize the projects and reminded me that the money was important and should be spent wisely. It also solidified my hatred for corruption because it meant that someone's tax money was wasted.

Keeping Everyone Safe, Our Way

As I had mentioned earlier, CAC did not hire a large security firm to manage our safety. Many programs spent up to 15 percent of their budget — millions of dollars — on security from large firms. The foreigners often would be driven around in armored vehicles that were obvious and stuck out from the typical vehicle. That may have been safer in some places, but it also made them a target. At CAC, we drove around in nondescript, common, beat-up vehicles that blended into the local traffic. It made us hidden in plain sight. We often dressed in local clothing and grew beards to blend in. We worked with local community leaders to hire trusted security guards, who were loyal to the leaders and us. We also treated them as part of the team rather than just paid help. They felt invested in the program. In addition, we worked with communities to get security guarantees from the local leaders before any project could start. Since we were doing that nonprofit, and just paying for labor and materials with no subcontractors making money off of the projects, the communities understood that the project was theirs, and its success depended upon them keeping the projects and people safe.

That security system worked very well for us. Through the entire length of the program, we never lost a single staff member, either foreigner or local Afghan. There was one member of our staff who was killed while at home in Khost, but we did not think that that had anything to do with our program. There were local insurgent issues in his area, and we thought that his family had some external problems that could have led to his death. We did have one local staff member in Laghman who was kidnapped for a short time, but our connections with the local community quickly led to a solution when the projects were shut down. The community essentially put together a posse to go and track down the perpetrators. When thousands of people were suddenly out of work due to some idiots kidnapping a staff member, the community would pull out all of the stops to ensure that the situation was fixed quickly. Within a few days, the staff member was released without harm, and the projects resumed immediately.

Almost Going to Jail ... Again

During the last few months of the program, the Afghanistan government was implementing new rules on security companies in Afghanistan. The new rules were going to prohibit foreign private security companies from operating in Afghanistan. I think that was due to two reasons. First, some foreign security companies had become very heavy handed with local citizens, and people were fed up being treated poorly in their own country. Second, and probably the main reason, was that many aid agencies were paying huge sums of money to those private security companies, and the government wanted that money for itself. At first, it had very little impact on our program, because we did not hire any private security companies. We simply chose our own local security guards and had an expat leader for each team in every province. We also got permission from the governors to carry weapons, so no one really bothered us. That was not normal for aid agencies, so it was hard to see where we would fit in to the new rules.

In the last few months of our program, a police truck showed up at our gate and demanded to be let in. Our American security leader let the truck in and then came to my office to get me. The new Nangarhar provincial police chief was there and demanded that I come to the governor's office, and that I was under arrest for having illegal weapons. Again, the security leader thought that I was in big trouble, but I was not worried. I calmly got in the back seat of the truck with my interpreter, and they drove me down to the governor's compound. They escorted me into the building and the police chief told me to wait outside of the deputy governor's office while he went in to tell them that I was there. Governor Sherzai was ill, and the deputy governor was assuming his duties at the time. The deputy governor, Mohammad Khan, was actually an old friend of mine who had been the director of education for many years. We had built schools together back when I was in the Army, and we had formed a good relationship over the years.

The police chief finally came to fetch me after about 10 minutes and sounded like he was very happy to be arresting me. As I walked in Mohammad Khan was looking down at some papers he was signing. The police chief told Mohammad Khan that I was there, and as he looked up from his desk he smiled and greeted me with a big hug and asked me how I had been. He quickly called in a young boy and instructed him to get tea and candy for us. The chief's jaw dropped, and he sat there for at least 15 minutes stewing, while Mohammad Khan and I talked about our families and successful projects we had done over the years. After a few laughs, Mohammad Khan turned to the police chief to ask him what the meeting was all about. The chief told him that we had weapons for our security that were not authorized under the new rules. I explained to Mohammad Khan how we had been doing our security for the last few years and that we were going to be closing down the project in a few months. I really did not want to go through a lot of changes, since we were leaving soon anyway. Mohammad Khan agreed and told me just to turn in our weapons to the police chief at the end of the program, and it would be fine. The chief lightened up and agreed. I think he just wanted our weapons anyway. The police chief dropped me back off at our compound, and our security leader seemed surprised to see me. He said he was sure that I was going to be in jail, and he was going to be calling Singapore to try to tell the boss that I was gone.

Living in a Very Different Culture

Living and working in Afghanistan was an eye-opening experience from a cultural standpoint. As a dominantly Muslim country, there were the typical rules, such as no eating pork, no drinking alcohol (although the foreigners did), no personal contact between men and Afghan women, no homosexuality, and strict daytime fasting rules during the holy month of Ramadan. Although those were very strict rules, and everyone claimed to follow them, it turned out that many Muslims are just as hypocritical as Christians. During the month of Ramadan, everyone must fast between dawn and dusk. However, on more than one occasion, one of my Afghan staff members would come into my office and grab a granola bar off of my desk and devour it quickly, saying, "I hate fasting crap." One of my Afghan colleagues for many years preached a lot to me about Islam and claimed to be a strict follower of the rules, but years later while visiting my office in Kabul I asked him if I could offer him a water or soda. He looked around for a second and quietly said, "Have you got any beer?"

The issue of homosexuality was always a volatile one in Afghanistan. No Afghan would ever want to admit that sex between men happens in there, but it is an open secret that young boys are raped by older boys/men at a large percentage. In a candid conversation with one of my Afghan friends, he told me that, even though it is illegal, about 30 percent of boys are raped. I could not believe it and asked him why he thought that was. He told me, "Well, we have urges!" It is not something that anyone likes to talk about, but hiding the issue does little to stop it. Most Afghan men, outside of the major cities anyway, have little to no interaction with females once they reach close to puberty and begin wearing full body-covering burkas. Perhaps that lack of sexual outlet leads to that behavior in males, but what do I know? Afghan men often do not have an opportunity to have any legal sexual interaction with women until marriage. Marriages are commonly arranged by the family, and it is customary to marry first cousins. That keeps families tied together and also assures that assets stay in the family. Although that might seem strange to Westerners, it is commonplace in Afghanistan. Those observations are not merely my thoughts but came directly from my Afghan friends.

"Slate" Magazine Visit

About halfway through my year as senior program manager, a journalist working for "Slate" magazine came to our compound to interview me and a few other members of our eastern region team. She had heard about our work and wanted to get the scoop on how we were doing business compared to other development agencies. Her piece was decent and reflected a lot of our feelings about what we were doing in Afghanistan, but she really wanted to put a spotlight on the military angle. Since most of the guys on our team were ex-military and not the typical Peace Corps volunteer-type of person, she was interested in seeing how we were operating differently. There was a running joke that we were "development mercenaries," and some scoffed at the lack of formal education our team members had. I simply pointed out that our team was made up of guys who understood how to get the job done and knew that failure was not an option. I was not trying to say that others were not capable of doing the job, but some people took it that way.

Get to Dubai Now!

Later in the year I was on a periodic visit to the Kandahar region when I got a call from Stan. He wanted me to get to Dubai to discuss some issues. I was going to cut my trip to Kandahar short and head to Dubai straight from there. I was very busy the night before and did not catch the news that a moronic pastor in Florida had used his tiny congregation to incite rage in the Muslim world by burning Korans. Burning or intentionally destroying the Holy Koran books are seen as an egregious act by Muslims and often causes huge backlash. Little did I know the next morning that residents of the city of Kandahar were going to be protesting and rioting in response to that Florida pastor's actions.

I was supposed to be heading to the airport when the local police told us to stay put in our compound due to the danger of riots against Westerners that day. It was going to be tough to fly out. I called Stan and told him there was something weird going on in the city. He shouted at me, "Where is your situational awareness? Don't you know what is happening with the Koran burnings? Pay attention and get here!" One of the guards said that he had a friend in the police who could escort us to the airport, and I thought that might be okay. I was in for the ride of my life. The young police officer pulled up in a police truck, and told me to throw my luggage in the back and hop in. He reeked of marijuana but was very persistent. I jumped in the truck, and we headed out on the 30-minute trip to the airport.

Along the way, there were tires burning and roads blocked, with people shouting and swinging sticks. It seemed that every major road was blocked with rioters. The whole town was black with smoke from the fires, and as we drove on it seemed that we would not make it. After driving wildly fast through alleyways and side streets, we came upon a burning roadblock on the only road to the airport. The driver just looked at me and laughed. He pulled out his pistol and started firing out the window into the air as he launched the truck through the burning tires. We made it through, and the rioters scattered as he shot into the air. I remember laughing and just shaking my head thinking, "So this is how I am going to die, wow!" After we made it through the last roadblock, we were out of the city, and it was a smooth ride the rest of the way. I made my flight and gave the police officer some money for his help. There was no way I would have made it without him.

When I got to Dubai, I was not exactly sure what Stan wanted to talk about. We met with one of the tribal chiefs that was a friend of Stan's and some other guys who worked for other U.S. government agencies. It seemed like Stan just wanted to catch up with me and give me a breather for a couple of days. A couple of the other guys from the company, who were running some smaller programs in Afghanistan, were also there. We all met for drinks at a swanky bar at the top of one of the hotels in Dubai and discussed how our programs were doing. Out of the blue, one of the guys mentioned that the Taliban was tracking me and had put a $200,000 price on my head. Apparently they had the idea that I was some kind of spy, probably because I was ex-military. I kind of chuckled but then started to be a little concerned. I asked Stan if he knew about it. He said, "Of course, but don't worry. We talked to the Taliban through our tribal connections, and they understand what you are doing. They aren't going to touch you." As comforting as that was to hear that, I was a bit worried and it would certainly cut down the amount of time that I would spend out in the rural areas. I was beginning to think that maybe Stan pulled me out to Dubai for a little while to get me out of there, while his connections talked to the Taliban and got things sorted out. I never knew what Stan was thinking, and maybe that was a good thing.

Losing Another Friend

Unfortunately, not everyone in Afghanistan was as lucky. During the year, one of our friends Linda Norgrove, who was working on a different

USAID project, was kidnapped while driving to an event in the province of Kunar. She was later killed during a rescue attempt by the U.S. military. It was a shock and sad time for everyone. Linda was the type of person who would never harm a soul. She had a kindness to her that made her perfect for her job in international development. She deeply cared about what she was doing, and it showed in her every action. Losing a person like Linda in such a traumatic way was a blow to all of us in the community.

Staying Sane with Vacations

One of the perks of working in Afghanistan was the ability to take a lot of vacation time and travel to places that are much harder to reach from the United States. Those breaks every couple of months were needed to unwind and forget about the stress of the program for a while. My favorite place to go was Southeast Asia. A few friends and I took a two-week vacation to Bali, Indonesia, and did some great partying and SCUBA diving, and even tried surfing. I also got to visit beautiful tropical islands in Thailand, Malaysia, and the Maldives. Those breaks allowed me to recharge my batteries and keep my sanity, but, of course, I still was always checking my emails every night, because it seemed that there was always something weird going on every time I left the country.

Keeping Everybody Happy

With so many projects happening at once all over the country, I felt like half of my job was trying to keep everyone happy. Our donor, USAID, wanted constant updates, and I would go to Kabul at least every six weeks to keep them updated on our progress. My goal was to brief them and push information to them as much as possible to prevent them from pelting me with constant questions. It seemed to work great. Our USAID program representative that year was a terrific American named Dan. He was a true diplomat who was soft spoken and smart. We developed a great relationship. He appreciated the work that we did, and was always honest and straightforward with me about his expectations and how well we were meeting them. At the end of the year, Dan seemed to be very happy with what we had accomplished.

Keeping my boss, Stan, happy was a full-time job. Stan liked to always know what was going on in the provinces, which was fine. Unfortunately, Stan liked to contact provincial managers directly to discuss their issues. They would often open up and tell Stan about problems that never were told to me, so when Stan would call me and ask why some problem was happening in a particular province I was sometimes blindsided, since I had not been made aware of the problem. That drove me nuts. As a former military officer, I was used to a strict chain of command. Young Soldiers were not supposed to go around their commanders and complain to the general about a problem they had without first telling their superiors about it. Most people followed that same process, but a few seemed to enjoy venting to the big boss and letting me get beat up for it. Despite silly things like that, Stan and Rani were very happy with the work we did. At the end of the year, I thanked Rani for the opportunity they gave me to run the program. She said, "No, I want to thank you for the great program you guys ran." That would always stick with me.

Keeping the Afghans happy was also a challenge. No matter how much work that we did, it was never going to be enough to satisfy the needs out in the provinces. Afghanistan's infrastructure was so destitute and outdated that it would take 20 times the amount of work that we had completed to put a dent in the needs that the country had. Unfortunately, there was never a good master plan to really address the issues. We were putting bandages on a 10-year hemorrhage at that point, and it seemed like that was going to be business as usual for the future. The work we had done certainly revitalized several areas of the country, and many Afghans very much appreciated the work. I know we had made a huge difference in the lives of thousands of people, and I think I can rest satisfied, knowing we had done a great thing for the people of Afghanistan.

Closing Down

When the year ended, USAID let us know that our funding was going to be cut significantly, and we were going to have to close most of our provincial offices. Closing them was a big job, since all finance books had to be reconciled, money needed to be moved, weapons had to be turned in to the local police, and office equipment had to be moved to other USAID programs or donated to local government departments. I built a closedown checklist and flew around the country to personally work with provincial managers to close down as many sites as possible. It allowed me to ensure that things were completed right, and gave me a chance to say goodbye and thank the managers for their amazing work. On the trip around the provinces, we also went out to take one last look at several of the projects and chat with some local leaders about how the program went. Many leaders were sad to see the program end and begged us to keep it going. Of course, we had no power to make that choice. Thirteen of the provincial offices were closing down; only six in the southern provinces would remain open for the next year and at significantly reduced budgets. My part in rebuilding Afghanistan was finally done.

Moving to Dubai

I had planned to go to graduate school at the end of the year, since the program had shrunk, and I did not feel that I was needed anymore. I was accepted to a graduate program in Bangkok, Thailand, for international development and was excited to move on to a new place. However, Stan and Rani asked me if I would like to stay with the company and try to take our program approach to other countries in Africa and the Middle East, while still overseeing the then smaller Afghanistan program. I agreed and moved to Dubai for the next year, where I would be based. Dubai was a good place to be, since it was only a two-hour flight to Afghanistan and only a few hours flight to most east African countries that the company was thinking of focusing on.

I traveled at least two weeks out of each month. I spent at least one week in Afghanistan and one week in another country. The Afghanistan program pretty much mirrored a smaller version of what we had done the year before. The leadership that took over the program in-country was well trained, and continued the same systems that we had put in place and improved upon them. It was pretty much on autopilot, so I was able to just check in with the team and help in case of any issues. I worked with Stan to try to focus on other countries, but the company did not have a defined strategy of what to do. Stan was not sure where he wanted to focus his attention, and it seemed like we were just throwing darts at the map trying to decide where to go. I traveled to Kenya, Somalia, Yemen, and South Sudan looking for opportunities, but since USAID was the main donor of our type of program, and all of the decisions were made in Washington, D.C., it seemed as though we were just talking to people who could not make decisions anyway.

Yemen — A Little Off Topic

The craziest trip I took was to Yemen, where CAC had opened a small office in the capital of Sanaa. The company was looking to focus on agricultural products, like honey production, there. I went to meet with the USAID deputy chief of mission to brief him on our program in Afghanistan and to see if they would be willing to fund a similar program for southern Yemen, where government forces had pushed Al Qaeda forces out of some of the major towns. The briefing went very well, but it did not look like much would come of it. We were scheduled to fly back to Dubai the next day, but then Stan pulled me aside and told me he had set up a separate plan for me to fly down to the southern part of Yemen and tour the devastation from the fighting firsthand. That was pretty crazy since no western civilians were going there at the time due to security issues. The towns had just been liberated from the fighting mere days before, and it was very dangerous and unstable, so who better to send than me! He told me that I would fly down to the main city of Aden, meet up with some of our company's friends, and they would take me to the devastated cities.

The next day I flew into Aden with no idea what to expect. Two guys, wearing button-down shirts, and what could only be described as towels wrapped around their waists and torn-up flip-flops, picked me up in a beat-up truck. Aden was, at the time, a nice-looking place with a new airport and good roads. They took us to an old Sheraton Hotel that looked like it had been abandoned for years. It was dirty and old, but I could not have cared less. The guys stayed up all night, singing and chewing on khat, a stimulant weed common in that part of the world, that they pack inside of their cheeks like tobacco. I did not know how they were going to be ready the next morning to travel, but they were. I first had to go to the small U.S. military post in Aden to talk to the U.S. Navy SEAL team that was stationed there to work with the local military. I briefed them on where I was going, and they kind of looked at me like I was nuts. They were not even allowed to go to those dangerous towns, and THEY WERE SEALS! They worried a bit about me, so they said they would get one of the Yemen Army colonels to go with me. I happily agreed. They asked me to take pictures so that they could see what was going on there.

Within an hour, I was on the road with my guys and a local colonel to drive out to the hot zone. On the way to the towns, we stopped to see the exiled governor of the province that we were going to. He was shocked to see a white guy driving around that war-torn area. I told him through my interpreter that I came to see the devastation to note if there was anything our company could do to help. I told him that I worked for a company called CAC. He immediately said, "CIA???" I quickly corrected him, "No, CAC, I'm not with the government." He seemed unconvinced. In his mind, any white guy trolling around there had to be a spy. I did not blame him. CIA certainly would have made more sense than what I was doing. He obliged and just told me to be careful, since the areas were still not clear of land mines and booby traps that Al Qaeda left behind as they fled. How nice! I thanked him, and we moved along.

As we got closer to the towns that we wanted to see, it was clear that Al Qaeda had destroyed as much of the infrastructure as they could during their retreat. Power lines were deliberately cut between poles, and several power poles were blown up out of the ground. When we reached the first town we were greeted by local militia reluctant to let us through the checkpoint. The colonel, whom we had brought along, was very helpful in getting us access. As we drove through the town it was clear to see that the devastation was vast. Some still-smoldering buildings had been leveled to the ground from huge bombs. Buildings that remained standing had been peppered with bullet holes. Doors and windows had been blown in. Debris from the bombed-out buildings littered the streets like something out of a World War II picture of Berlin. Pretty much every building had been destroyed. It was surreal. There were spray-painted messages on the roads, with arrows pointing in certain directions. I asked the colonel what they said. He calmly claimed, "They say there are land mines that way, so we shouldn't go that way." I laughed and nodded with a grin.

We stopped on the side of the road in the middle of town where there had been a small shop and house that were both leveled. There was a family that looked confused and distraught sitting outside of the destroyed shop. We asked them what they were doing there. They told us that that was their house and store. They had lost everything and had no idea what they were going to do. I grabbed some water out of the truck and offered it to them. We sat and talked for a while. They showed me some of the huge .50 caliber machine gun rounds that were left on the ground in front of the shop, and told me how the place had been so peaceful years ago and that their family had been there for generations. My heart just sank. I tried to put myself in their shoes and imagine something like that happening to my family. We gave them whatever food we had along and thanked them for talking with us. We visited two towns that were both similar to that, and then we went back to Aden, where I showed the SEAL team the pictures and briefed them on the situation. I was eager to get back to Sanaa and talk to the embassy and USAID.

I arrived back in Sanaa the next day, and as soon as I reached my hotel room a representative from the U.S. Defense Attaché office called me and asked if he could come to my hotel room to see the pictures that I had taken of the devastation. The USAID representative called, as well. Since I was the only Westerner crazy enough to go down there, everyone wanted to hear about what I had seen. The Defense Attaché representative came right away to my hotel room and was taken aback by the amount of destruction. I set up a meeting with the USAID representative who worked on emergency projects for Yemen. I showed him the photos and told him that I could put together a proposal to start working in the affected area right away. I also told him that I could have boots on the ground in a week, hiring hundreds of people to start clearing the rubble and restoring basic services as quickly as possible. There were people who had lost everything and needed work, money, and food right away. We were in a position to make that happen quickly if USAID would just green light the funding. The USAID representative had worked in Afghanistan and was well aware of our program there, so he knew what we could do. Unfortunately, red tape and agreements with other companies prevented him from doing anything. Nothing came of it, and within the next two years Yemen descended into an all-out civil war that turned into one of the worst famines in recent history.

U.S. Military in Kabul

In addition to our attempts to push our programs into other developing countries in the region, our main focus remained in Afghanistan. Since the USAID program had shrunk, I focused on other possible areas, such as Kabul, where the U.S. military had tens of millions of dollars to do some work but had absolutely no idea what to do with it. I took over negotiations with the major from one of our other managers, who was focusing his efforts on Somalia. The U.S. military liked our approach and the success that we had had in other areas of the country and wanted to fund similar projects in the capital city. They did not really know where to start, and the major in charge of the program — and the funding — never really left his base, so he was clueless about the needs of the community.

I tried to help him by providing some ideas of infrastructure needs that would be easy to tackle in a comprehensive way so that he could get the most bang for the buck with their funds. One of the first areas that I showed him was the awful road conditions in neighborhoods around Kabul. Even in the rich areas of the city, many of the roads were practically not drivable due to huge holes and uneven gravel. The ditches by the roads, which were both rain gutters and sewers from the houses, were either clogged or destroyed, leaving huge puddles of human sewage covering the unkept roads. It was both a major health hazard and traffic problem in an overcrowded city. That was one area where their money could be spent and would make a significant impact. All they had to do was say go, and we could get to work on it immediately, working with the government and communities.

The discussions on starting work with the U.S. military went on for months. The major needed approval from his leadership, but they never gave it. Just like prior military units in Nangarhar that I had dealt with years before, it seemed like everyone wanted to talk, but no one wanted to be responsible to act. The major I was working with finally came to the end of his tour in Afghanistan and was replaced by another major, an accountant by trade, who did not share any appetite to do projects. He decided that the best way to spend money was to provide advisors to the Afghanistan government's Ministry of Economy. I told him that the minister already had technical advisors from at least six different countries working with him. Adding another one would be futile. In the end, nothing actually happened, and we decided not to waste any more time dealing with the U.S. military in Kabul. It was yet another wasted opportunity to do some good, but instead we squandered it.

Ring Road Fiasco

Around the same time that we were trying to work with the military, we started working with a U.S. company that was contracted to construct a major highway project through the western Afghanistan province of Badghis. That was the last portion of the "ring road," which was the major highway that connected all of Afghanistan by forming a complete ring around the country. It was the main roadway for moving all goods and services in the country, but one portion remained to be built. A Chinese company had attempted to build it years before but had a tough time working with the Afghans, and they ended up being attacked many times, causing deaths and destroyed equipment. The government needed it built, and a large American/Turkish contactor was hired and needed someone to do community development around the area to help get local communities on board. We were a perfect fit for that kind of work.

I was working on that project with Bahar, who had been the manager in Nimroz the year before, where he had built dams and huge irrigation projects. He was a great partner to have on that one since he was an Afghan and knew very well how to work best with the government and communities. The construction company did not know much about community development and getting local buy-in, so they left that planning up to us. They gave us a $2 million budget that we could use to do local infrastructure projects. Since we had worked in Badghis over the last year on our other program we knew what to do. We started mapping out the areas for what was needed and formed a community engagement plan to start talking to the local district councils. It was going to be an exciting year, we thought.

Even before the project started there seemed to be all kinds of issues dealing with the Afghanistan Ministry of Public Works. The minister did not like our approach to conducting community development directly with the communities. He wanted us to hire subcontractors to do individual projects, almost exclusively to build mosques. It was obvious what he wanted to do: hire his preferred contractors on a few projects that he could get kickbacks on. That was pretty standard in Afghanistan, where everyone expected to get some money out of it. Building a handful of mosques in the area might sound nice to someone who has no clue, but it would create very few jobs, cause a lot of infighting in the communities, and do little to benefit the communities directly. We tried hard to lobby the minister on that and show him the benefits of our approach, but it was pretty obvious what his motivations were. Everyone could see it, but there was little we could do about it. We hoped we could convince him to change his mind once the road construction started.

The construction company's road crew began conducting the survey of the road and were threatened and attacked. The construction company realized they were going to have a lot of problems getting the community on board with the project. They turned to us, since we had experience building roads in difficult areas of the country and asked how we would do it. We told them that we would not rely on using heavy equipment to build the road through the village areas. Instead we would rely on manual labor from the local villages to cut and fill the road by hand, creating thousands of jobs and getting the community involved rather than bring in large excavators that would destroy a lot of their land, with them gaining minimum benefit from the project directly. The company asked if we would take on the task of mobilizing the community to cut and fill the road by hand. All of the finishing work would be done by heavy equipment later after the community was already involved with the parts that could be done manually. We agreed but, of course, would need to have an amended contract to do it.

Just when I thought we were going to get moving on the project several delays started. There were security issues, government interference issues, and other contractual problems. We were getting frustrated but were willing to be patient. The construction company decided to modify our contract that had some significant problems with it. That frustrated Stan, and we considered just ending our relationship with them, since it was becoming too much of a pain and was not worth the effort. A representative from the construction company came over to my house to work things out with me. He seemed to be under the impression that we were some kind of weak subordinate that he could intimidate. I was surprised when he told me that he was there to get us to agree to some new terms to our contract. When I politely told him that we were not interested in his new terms, as they were unacceptable, he sternly told me, "You guys are going to do this!" I sternly struck back, "No, we won't be doing any of this. Perhaps you need to find someone else if this is the way you treat your partners. You can show yourself out." I think that guy had a tough meeting with his boss after losing us as a subcontractor, because later that night I got a call from the head of the program, who was very unhappy to see us walk away. They really needed our help, but we were certainly not going to be treated like crap for very little gain. In the end, the project was scrapped, and as of the writing of this book the road was never built. Yet another wasted opportunity to do some good.

Time to Move On

After a year of living in Dubai and running back and forth to Afghanistan and other places, I was exhausted and ready to make a change. The company was not sure what direction it wanted to go, and I felt that with no real strategy I was not able to focus my attention and be of much value. I recently got married and my wife and I decided to leave and go to Kenya for a few months. We went on great safaris and enjoyed spending time with some old friends who were there. We looked at work opportunities in Kenya, but not much came of it. We decided to go to Romania, my wife's home, for a while and take a break. We spent so little time together over the past year that it was nice to take some time for ourselves. But after about five months off it was time to get back to work

CHAPTER 4. BACK TO AFGHANISTAN ONE MORE TIME

In June of 2013, an opportunity came up at DBS International in Afghanistan. I had previously written handbooks for the military while under contract from DBS, so I was familiar with the company. The company was looking for someone to be the manager of a training program for the Afghanistan Peace and Reconciliation Program (APRP) for a year. The APRP project was a U.S. military-sponsored group that worked with local governments and communities to try to bring back Afghan men who had joined the Taliban and other insurgent groups and reintegrate them into their communities. Our job involved creating and implementing a training program for the local APRP staff members who did the various jobs related to the program.

When the program first started, the APRP staff members who were hired had very little training for their jobs. Those included: finance, monitoring, peace negotiation, leadership, and others. As the program manager, I would need to hire local staff members who could build training modules and then actually conduct training of the APRP staff. Since it was a U.S. military-funded project I would also need to deal with the local U.S. Army captain, who was the contracting officer for the program. I had never run a capacity training program before, but it seemed pretty straightforward. Just like anything else I could figure it out and with a lot of help would build a system to manage the program. I applied and accepted the job, and within a couple of weeks I was on my way back to Kabul, Afghanistan.

Life in Kabul

Living and working in Kabul was very different from being out in the provinces. Kabul was a big, overpopulated city, with plenty of poverty but also plenty of wealth. There were bars and restaurants that Westerners could go to and eat, drink, and party like anywhere else. Most of those restaurants were heavily guarded and fortified with 15-foot walls around them for protection. They were obvious targets for any insurgent group to attack. Many Westerners traveled around in armored trucks for protection, which was much different from my years of driving around in nondescript cars, trying to blend into the population.

My company had four U.S. citizens working in Afghanistan at that time, including me. The other three worked for a separate U.S. military contract, and I was on my own as the only full-time U.S. citizen for my program. We all lived on a large hotel compound called The Baron. The Baron housed hundreds of Westerners. It was fortified with blast walls and armed Nepalese guards, and had everything we needed as a self-contained town. It had a gym, racquetball courts, gardens, two restaurants, bars, stores, a travel agency, and even a barbershop. Life was pretty easy on the compound. Every morning the Westerners would head out to their offices spread out all over the city and then return later in the evening, when everyone would get together for dinner, drinks, and leisure time. Everyone made friends and tried to enjoy our time locked up in our little prison for the year. Although we lived pretty well for Afghanistan, it was hard not to get lonely. Days were spent in the same basic routine: get up, go to work, eat, relax, work out, watch the five TV channels that broadcast in English, and go to bed. We kicked back and had drinks and relaxed a few times a week, but I missed my wife a lot, and partying was not really my thing.

Our company office was located across town on the south side of Kabul. That meant that each morning we would need to commute about an hour through jammed Kabul traffic. The city was never built to handle so much traffic, and since there were few traffic rules that anyone followed it was always a mess getting back and forth. The police set up checkpoints all over the city, supposedly to check for Taliban and insurgents trying to infiltrate the city. However, those police checkpoints really seemed to be there more to annoy Westerners. Not every vehicle was stopped, but we were constantly stopped and checked for weapons. It was pretty common to see cars full of more-suspicious looking men drive right through a checkpoint in front of us, only to have the police stop us, and check our vehicles for guns that could be confiscated and sold for money. We did not have any weapons on us, so it was a waste of time, but it always made me wonder if those police officers were interested in keeping the city safe or just trying to make a quick buck. As the city became more and more unstable, those things bothered me regularly.

Why Are We Doing This Again???

After getting settled, I attended my first meeting with the Afghan APRP executive staff, the U.S. military contracting officer, and a few other U.S. government representatives. The meeting went a lot different than I thought it would. The Afghans were apparently not aware that the program was going to be happening. The Afghans had asked for the training over two years prior, when the APRP project was first started. By this point, the program had been running for years and was actually under threat of being defunded by the new U.S. military commander in Afghanistan. It took the U.S. military over two years to finally get the program funded and contracted out to us. The Afghans felt that the training was kind of useless at the current point. I had to kind of chuckle, since I knew how inefficient the military was at getting funding and contracts approved. The contracting officer just kind of nodded and said, "Well, we got the contract now, so we might as well use it. Maybe it will still be of value." He was new to Afghanistan himself, and that program was started well before he got there. He was just trying to run the contract he was given.

Even though I knew the program might be almost useless, we still drove on working to create the best training program that we could. The way we looked at it was that we were helping to build capacity in the local population regardless of when it would be used. If we trained people in those skills, and they would use the skills to help benefit a future business or other development program, that would still help add value to the country. It was time to get to work on creating the program.

Building a New Program

In order to accomplish our goal of building a successful training program, we needed to hire good local trainers who were experts in their areas. My company had partnered with another company on the program, and together we found a good mix of guys. I brought in three of my old colleagues from the community development program that I had run in 2012. The other company brought in three of its well-known colleagues from past programs, and we recruited for some part-time trainers on other specific topics. We also hired two part-time American ladies who helped to build the training manuals and write some content on peace building in Afghanistan. They were both awesome people, who I had nothing but respect for. We got along great, and they did a superb job. It turned out to be a good team all around. Over the next year, we all worked to build a training program and training manuals to go with it. At the end of the year, we conducted several large training seminars at a local hotel conference room for hundreds of APRP staff members, who flew in from every province of Afghanistan.

Finishing Out the Program

After the training seminars were done, I met with the Afghan official who was in charge of the APRP program. I hated dealing with that particular guy, because he seemed to do very little in his job but was always complaining about something. I gave him a final briefing on our program and handed him copies of our final training manuals that they could use to help do follow-up on training if they wanted to. I knew those training manuals would never be opened again.

The office that guy had was in an old building that had been lavishly restored by the U.S. government. It had beautiful, ornate furnishings, and the entire building was clad in white marble. I could not help but ponder how much money was wasted on that building that could have gone to much-needed infrastructure projects in the provinces.

After my briefing was over, we had a cordial conversation about the state of things in Afghanistan. It was clear to me that he had no idea what was happening in the provinces and how impoverished the country truly was. Instead he started pointing out small flaws in the construction of the building. He showed me where there were rust stains on the white marble façade of the building. He said the reconstruction was not very good, and that some donor should come in and redo the work. I bit my tongue, but I really wanted to shake the guy and explain to him that it was insane to build palaces in Kabul instead of roads and irrigation for the destitute people in provinces. The conversation showed how disconnected those government officials were from the real issues that needed solving in their country.

Shutting Down

As the year drew to a close, we waited to see if the U.S. military wanted to continue the contract or just cut the APRP program along with our training. We had a conclusion meeting with the general who was in charge of the funding for pretty much all of the military programs, including the APRP program. When I arrived at the military headquarters, I was happy to see one of my old friends, Jonathan. We went to college together and were roommates when we were both young platoon leaders in the 82nd Airborne Division 10 years before. He was working on the general's staff and told me a little about what to expect when we briefed the general. I was the only one in the room who was not in the Army and wearing civilian clothes. The contracting officers for the APRP program were there, as well, to brief the general on the program, and I was just there in case there were any questions about my program.

The meeting went quickly. In 2014, the Obama administration was looking to draw down U.S. forces, so anything that could be cut or turned over to the Afghan government was most likely going to be defunded. I had little hope that our program would be saved, and in all honesty if I had to make the decision I would have canceled our program. The big takeaway from the briefing was that the APRP program had helped bring about 10,000 low-level fighters back into their communities. I thought that was pretty impressive actually. The contracting officers who were briefing the general seemed to have little understanding of their own program. When the general asked them simple questions about the effectiveness of the APRP program, the officers struggled to give any coherent answers. They seemed to be very nervous briefing the general, which was not uncommon for young officers. I wanted to jump in and help, but I knew it was not my place to talk unless I was directly asked a question. In the end, the general killed the entire APRP program and our training program along with it. My job was effectively done.

Kabul Starts to Deteriorate

After the fall of the Taliban from 2002 until 2014, Kabul had been a relatively safe place to be. Westerners could walk around the streets, shop at the markets, eat, and party pretty freely without much worry about security. Although people took precautions, it was fairly unusual to see a major attack in Kabul. It only happened a couple of times a year. That began to change in the 2014 time frame and got progressively worse. In 2014, the Taliban attacked my favorite Lebanese restaurant, Taverna. People from 10 different countries were killed or injured in the attack, and the place never recovered. The owner of the restaurant was a popular Lebanese man who was always happy to see us, served us huge portions, and always made us feel like family. He was among the 14 people killed in the attack. I had actually wanted to eat there that night and was glad I had not. Several hotels and compounds, like the one I was living at, were attacked by large car bombs to breach the walls and then followed up by gunfire from insurgents coming in through the breach. The attacks have only increased over the years.

Time to Get Out

As I closed down the program and said goodbye to my friends and colleagues, I was happy to finally head home and put Afghanistan behind me. I had lived the majority of my life in Afghanistan for nearly a decade. I put my heart and soul into that country, and I truly believe that my efforts made a significant difference in the lives of many people there. I did start up and oversee a couple of other programs for Afghanistan from the Washington, D.C., area in 2015, but I only needed to do a couple of short visits. Kabul was deteriorating, and with a wife and soon a child on the way I was happy to leave Afghanistan in my rearview mirror. I still keep in contact with some of my Afghan friends who are living through the tough times there and are hoping for change. It breaks my heart a bit to hear how bad it is getting in areas that were once relatively safe. There is really no telling what will happen in Afghanistan in the future. I felt that I did the best that I could to help advance peace and prosperity there, and the rest is in God's hands.

Lessons Learned

The years that I had spent in Afghanistan taught me many lessons about the way our government works in wartime and during a military occupation. First, we have to treat the occupied population with dignity and respect. It is their country, and we are there temporarily. Winning hearts and minds only happens when we are working in partnership with the local population and have their trust.

Second, we have to get better at the way we do rebuilding in a conflict zone, like Afghanistan. The U.S. spent billions of dollars in an effort to rebuild Afghanistan, but we approached it poorly. That was mainly due to the fact that there was no real master plan for rebuilding. We did a series of programs dealing with everything from education to agriculture, but many programs failed because they were not designed with good input from seasoned veterans on the ground. That led to a massive waste of time and money, and fueled corruption in Afghanistan. If we are ever to embark on another adventure like rebuilding Afghanistan, we need to design a solid, comprehensive plan early on that addresses the needs on the ground and truly solves major problems. The amount of money spent in Afghanistan could have solved many of those issues, but instead most was wasted.

Last, it does not matter how big of an army we have or how long we stay, Afghanistan will have to choose its own path. There was a saying that I heard many times from Afghans: "You may have the watches, but we have the time." It may take generations of time for Afghanistan to truly become a stable nation. The country has endured 40 years of instability and conflict. It will only turn around when Afghans can admire their leaders, respect their tribal and ethnic diversity, trust in the rule of law, and gain at least some economic prosperity throughout the country. It will be up to the Afghans to make that happen. We can help, but ultimately it will be their collective choice.

ABOUT THE AUTHOR

Chris Corsten is a former U.S. Army officer, civilian counternarcotics advisor, and humanitarian aid worker who lived and worked in Afghanistan for nearly a decade from 2005-2015. He is most known for his work as the senior program manager for one of USAID's largest community development programs in Afghanistan. His work has been showcased on CNN and the CBS show "60 Minutes". Chris has also been featured in the online magazine "Slate" and appeared on a radio broadcast for NPR. His education includes a master's degree in sustainability from Harvard University Extension School, an MBA from the University of Maryland University College, and a bachelor's degree in biology from Ripon College.

Made in the USA
Monee, IL
22 May 2020